HOLIDAY HOMECOMING

HOME TO HEATHER CREEK

HOLIDAY HOMECOMING

Carolyne Aarsen

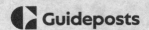

Home to Heather Creek is a trademark of Guideposts.

Copyright © 2023 by Guideposts. All rights reserved.

This book, or parts thereof, may not be reproduced, stored in a retrieval system, or transmitted in any form or by any means, electronic, mechanical, photocopying, recording, or otherwise, without the written permission of the publisher.

The characters and events in this book are fictional, and any resemblance to actual persons or events is coincidental.

Scripture references are from the following source: The Holy Bible, English Standard Version. ESV® Text Edition: 2016. Copyright © 2001 by Crossway Bibles, a publishing ministry of Good News Publishers.

Published by Guideposts Books & Inspirational Media
100 Reserve Road, Suite E200
Danbury, CT 06810
Guideposts.org

Cover by Lookout Design, Inc.
Interior design by Cindy LaBreacht
Additional design work by Müllerhaus
Typeset by Aptara, Inc.

ISBN 978-1-959634-66-9 (hardcover)
ISBN 978-1-959634-68-3 (epub)
ISBN 978-1-959634-67-6 (epdf)

Printed in the United States of America
10 9 8 7 6 5 4 3 2 1

Acknowledgments

Books are never written alone. They are a partnership and to that end, I would like to thank Fiona Serpa and Beth Adams for their wisdom and insight in helping me shepherd this book to publication. Thank you to Karen Solem, my agent, for her help, support and encouragement. I'd also like to thank my dear husband for putting up with vacant stares when story lines are dancing through my head—and late suppers when I'm trying to capture the stories on the page.

And finally, thanks to my children for being the wonderful people and amazing individuals you are. I hope the Slater children grow up to be like you!

—Carolyne Aarsen

Home to Heather Creek

Before the Dawn

Sweet September

Circle of Grace

Homespun Harvest

A Patchwork Christmas

An Abundance of Blessings

Every Sunrise

Promise of Spring

April's Hope

Seeds of Faith

On the Right Path

Sunflower Serenade

Second Chances

Prayers and Promises

Giving Thanks

Holiday Homecoming

HOLIDAY HOMECOMING

Chapter One

Of course the telephone would send out its shrill summons just as the timer for the oven went off. And of course Charlotte couldn't find her red oven mitts.

Her gaze skittered over the counter, the table half-covered with cookbooks and papers, but she could see no worn, red oven mitts.

She yanked open the oven door in the faint hope this would slow down the baking process. Then, belying her sixty-some years, she jogged across the worn linoleum and snatched the phone off the cradle.

"Hello," she said, breathless as she pushed a strand of graying hair back from her face, one eye on the cookies in the oven.

They looked done. She just hoped the caller wasn't her dear friend Hannah, whose phone calls could last up to half an hour when she was feeling chatty.

"Hello?" she said again as she realized the person on the other end hadn't replied to her greeting. "Hello?"

She shrugged and hung up the phone. Probably a telemarketer, she thought, wishing she had taken the time to slow down and look at the Caller ID before answering.

She wiped her hands on the bright yellow apron covering her worn shirt, glanced around the kitchen one more time, and then caught sight of her oven mitts tucked in behind a bag of flour on the wooden table.

She slipped them on her hands and then eased the perfectly browned cookies out of the oven and onto an overflowing counter.

To the casual onlooker, it might seem as if she were getting carried away with Christmas baking, but some of it was for the Bedford Gardens Convalescent Center. The residents there loved her baking as much as her own family did.

Christmas carols played from the radio in the living room, creating the sense of anticipation and wonder that came with the season.

Christmas was coming.

Charlotte had put out a few of her decorations in a bid to add to the ambience underlined by the scent of spices and chocolate wafting from the kitchen.

Sunshine sparkling on the snow outside only added to the feeling.

Christmas was coming, and now that her grandchildren were more settled into living on the farm, she hoped this year the holiday season would be full, rich, and peaceful.

Most of all she hoped for peaceful.

Life with three grandchildren in the house and a son who was getting married had made her and Bob's life busy and, at times, a bit frenetic.

But over the Christmas holidays the kids would be home from school and life would slow its pace, if only for a couple of weeks.

She put another pan of cookies in the oven, closed the door, and turned on the timer just as the telephone rang again. Once again she hurried to the phone, and once again there was only silence on the other end.

Prank call, she thought as she hung up, feeling slightly annoyed and a bit unsettled. Was it the same person who had previously called? And why the silence? If it was a wrong number, wouldn't they say so?

She went back to the radio in the living room off the kitchen and turned up the music to ease away the disquiet. Maybe it was a bit early to be listening to "The First Noel" and "Silent Night" in the first week of December, but she loved the atmosphere the songs created.

And once they went out and cut the Christmas tree this weekend, as Bob had promised they would, the piney scent would add another layer of Christmas to the house.

Her mind slipped back to last Christmas, their first with the children in the house. They had been understandably upset. After all, that was their first Christmas not only in a new place but also without their mother.

While struggling through their own loss, Charlotte and Bob had forced themselves to be strong for the kids.

At least they'd had the Christmas play. Though it had been a wonderful distraction, and though Charlotte had enjoyed seeing her grandchildren take part, she was thankful that this year they would all be willing spectators instead of participants.

She pulled the bag of flour off the kitchen table—and in the process knocked over an envelope that Sam had laid on the table the night before. A few papers slipped out, and as she caught sight of them she frowned.

Sam's college application forms.

Sam's *blank* college application forms.

She leafed through the papers, her heart growing heavier with each page she turned. Nothing had been filled in for any of the colleges he'd talked about applying to. In fact, one of the forms had a brown stain on the front. Spilled pop, most likely.

What was he thinking? Charlotte glanced over the papers once again and released an angry sigh. He had to have them filled in and sent by the end of the year to meet the deadline. He'd been dithering the past few months, and Charlotte had been struggling not to nag, but it looked as if she would have to give him yet another nudge.

She slid them into the envelope, her momentary feeling of well-being pushed aside. She hated nagging and for a moment was tempted to ask Bob to deal with it, but she knew how that scenario would play out.

Bob would ask Sam if he had filled out his forms. Sam would say no. Bob would say maybe he should. Sam would agree, and that would be the end of that scintillating discussion.

Sam's Uncle Pete might be one to light a fire under her grandson, but Charlotte didn't think it fair to put that kind of strain on her son. He was already stressed enough trying to figure out how the farm would pay for the house he needed to build for his future wife and Sam's college at the same time.

So it was up to her again.

"Something smells mighty good in here," Bob called out as he entered the porch. A blast of cool air accompanied his announcement, and Charlotte shivered.

"Do you want a cup of coffee?" she asked as she went to the cupboard for a mug. The question was simply rhetorical.

Bob always had a cup of coffee when he came into the house after doing his afternoon chores.

Didn't matter that in the winter the chores only consisted of walking through the cows, making sure their feed troughs were full, and checking on the horses. But chores were chores, and Bob tried to maintain the routine he had kept ever since he took over the farm from his father.

"Pretty nice out there today," he announced as he stepped into the kitchen, the light overhead glinting off his glasses and highlighting the gray strands in his thinning hair. "I think we're going to have a wonderful Christmas." He pulled out a handkerchief and blew his nose. His cheeks and the end of his nose were red in spite of the wonderful weather he was celebrating.

"That's three weeks away," Charlotte said, putting some cookies on a plate for him.

"I know, but according to our records, every time we've had nice weather the first week of December, it's been beautiful at Christmastime." Bob settled into his chair as Charlotte poured his coffee. The scent of hay and cold emanated from his clothes. "You're not having any?" he asked, glancing across the table to where she usually sat.

"I'm a little busy." Charlotte shot another glance at the clock.

"Surely you can spare a few minutes alone with your husband on a Friday afternoon before the kids come barging in. Lately it seems we haven't had much time to sit and chat."

The faint hurt in his voice hit her right in the guilt zone. Yes, she'd been busy lately, but that was the nature of family. Having Pete stay in the spare room since the tractor-shed fire damaged his apartment had added more work to her schedule as well. It seemed that busy was her default mode lately.

"I suppose I could." Charlotte didn't mean for the begrudging tone to enter her voice, but she could tell from the frown Bob shot her way that he had heard it.

"Of course, if you're too busy..."

"No. I'm not." She gave him a smile, pulled a mug out of the cupboard, and poured another cup of steaming coffee. Bob was right. The past few weeks had been busy, and with Christmas coming, more busy times lay ahead. They had to take their moments when they could.

As she settled in her usual chair, she gave him a quick smile and curled her hands around the warm mug. "How are the cows looking?"

"Good. Real good. Pete's been doing a great job with them. I think we're going to have a crackerjack batch of calves in the spring."

Charlotte smiled at Bob's unexpected compliment of their son. Though Pete was doing most of the physical labor on the farm, Bob still made the decisions and, unfortunately, the criticisms. It was nice to hear that he appreciated Pete's work.

Bob dunked a cookie in his coffee and as he took a bite, his elbow nudged the envelope Charlotte had set on the table, and it fell to the floor.

"What's this?" he asked, picking it up.

"Sam's college application forms."

"Are they ready to mail? Doesn't he need to send them out soon?"

"They need to be out by the end of the month, and no, they're not ready to mail. He hasn't filled anything in yet."

"What's the holdup?"

Charlotte shrugged. "I wish I knew. I've been after him to get them done for a while now."

Bob dropped the envelope on the crowded table. "He better get a move on." But that's all he said, and Charlotte knew it would be up to her.

"And I need to talk to Emily," Bob continued. "She was supposed to clean out the horse barn last week, but it's still looking pretty messy."

"I thought she said she did." Charlotte frowned, remembering Emily's vociferous complaints about the smell and the copious amount of manure she'd had to shovel out.

"Maybe she did, but she was supposed to keep an eye on it, and it's piling up again. Shouldn't let it go so far."

"I guess the kids still need reminders," Charlotte noted.

Bob shifted in his chair, frowned, pulled a sweater from the back of it, and tossed it aside. "Whose is this, and what's it doing here?"

"It's Christopher's. I told him to put it away last night. He must have forgotten."

"That boy's been getting more and more forgetful these days. He told me he'd checked the waterer for the horses, but when I checked it was frozen—and he didn't tell me."

"He's been busy," Charlotte said, though she knew her excuse was lame. Charlotte wanted to ask Bob why he had suddenly become so grumpy but decided to let it be. Sometimes the more she tried to dig into his moods the more he retreated.

Bob scratched his forehead with his thick, work-worn fingers and crossed his arms. As he leaned back, the old, wooden chair creaked with his weight. "Sometimes I feel like I'm a bit old for this."

Charlotte felt a tiny niggling of foreboding.

When they first took the children in, it had taken Bob a few months to adjust, but she knew he enjoyed having them around. Just the other day he had told Sam how much he appreciated his help. He and Christopher were talking about getting a 4-H animal for Christopher to enter in the fair. And though he liked to tease Emily about her clothing choices, Bob certainly had a soft spot for his granddaughter.

Then she had an idea that might explain his current funk.

"Is your blood sugar a bit high?" He often got a bit surly when that happened.

"Nope. Just been thinking." He sighed again, rocking a bit in his chair, making it creak with each movement. "I suppose I had pictured these years differently. I had seen us sitting back and enjoying the fruits of our labor. Relaxing, maybe doing a bit of traveling. You do realize that by the time Christopher is ready to graduate, we'll move right from here to the old folks' home."

Bob got up and took another couple of cookies from the pile cooling on the counter, and Charlotte decided to hold her tongue.

"Well, what's so wrong with that?" Charlotte asked.

On his way back to the table, Bob paused at the window and looked out over the yard. "I always thought that as Pete took on more of the farmwork, we'd have more time. The two of us."

"We have all day together," Charlotte reminded him, choosing to forget that only a few moments ago he'd had to ask her to join him in a cup of coffee. "And you're often visiting with your friends in town or hanging around the tractor supply anyway." And she didn't want to remind him that he had resisted Pete's slow takeover of the physical responsibilities of the farm, which gave him the free time.

Bob returned to the table and dropped into his chair again.

"I think we should take a trip someday. Just the two of us. Get away from here for a while. We never go anywhere."

"We went to San Diego to visit Denise, Kevin, and the children when they lived there."

"That wasn't traveling. That was visiting. And if you call sitting in that tiny apartment listening to Kevin go on and on about all the things he was going to do . . ." Bob snorted his anger. "Can't see what Denise saw in that blowhard. Couldn't stick around long enough to raise his own kids. Couldn't even show up for Denise's funeral." Another snort clearly stated his opinion on that as well.

Though Charlotte shared his anger with their absent son-in-law, she knew she couldn't express it aloud to Bob. Doing so would only pull both of them down into an ever-deeper spiral of frustration and bitterness.

Yes, Kevin had been a neglectful husband and father. Yes, he hadn't contacted the children since he left his family when Christopher was a baby, but she knew she had to keep her emotions about his actions buried. Kevin was still the children's biological father. As much as his actions, or rather inaction, bothered her, neither she nor Bob could let Sam, Emily, and Christopher see how they truly felt about him.

"If we were to take a trip, where would you want to go?" she said, latching onto his previous comment as a way of avoiding talking about Kevin.

Bob shrugged as he popped another cookie into his mouth. "Hawaii. Someplace warm."

Charlotte had to force herself to keep her mouth closed. She had a fairly vivid imagination, but it didn't extend far enough to imagine Bob lounging on a beach in Hawaii. A beach he would have to take an airplane to get to.

"I think that could be...fun," she said, opting to play along. "Although we'd have to make arrangements for the kids."

Bob rocked a bit more. "Yeah. The kids again. I suppose it was a silly idea."

"Not silly, exactly. It's just we need to do some advance planning and budgeting. We've got Pete and Dana's wedding coming up, and they have to find a place to live. And Sam's college education..." She let her voice trail off. She didn't want to think about how they would pay for all of that. The farm was holding steady, but extra money wasn't sitting around.

"It seems like there's always something with the kids."

"We had that with our own children as well," Charlotte gently reminded him.

"That's what I mean. We went through all that with Bill, Denise, and Pete. Now we're doing it again."

She didn't want to say anything to that. Didn't want to venture down the path he was headed toward. Instead she avoided the topic and took a sip of her coffee. Bob was just being Bob. Just voicing his complaints out loud, she reminded herself. She had to make sure not to make more of it than he did.

Christmas music flowed from the speakers, and the warmth of the corn-burner stove permeated the house along with the aroma of Christmas baking. But now the faintest sniggle of unease had entered the atmosphere.

"When is Anna supposed to have her baby?" Bob asked.

"Not for a couple more weeks. I hope after Bill gets back from Chicago. I know he hates to be away so close to her due date, but the meeting could mean a lot of grant money for River Bend."

The flash of sun reflecting off a window made her crane her neck to see a large, yellow school bus pull up out on the road, lights flashing as it came to a stop. Toby, their dog, let out a happy yelp as she streaked down the driveway toward the bus.

"The kids are home," Charlotte said, pushing her chair back as she stood.

Sam's car was broken down. Again. So he was on the bus today along with Emily and Christopher.

The bus doors swung open, and three bodies piled out. Sam, the eldest, was the first, and he immediately bent over, scooped up some snow, and packed it into a ball. Just behind him came his little brother, Christopher, his coat wide open, laces of his boots dragging, and his head bare.

He flung one hand over his head as Sam lobbed the snowball his way.

Emily was right behind Christopher, her arms full of books, her long blonde hair falling over her face as she ducked her head as well.

The snow hit her black, woolen coat, making a white blob that stuck.

Even through the windows, Charlotte could hear her granddaughter yelling at her brother. "Sam Slater, you are in such trouble!"

Toby danced around them all, a bundle of brown-and-black fur, her plume-like tail waving a welcome.

The doors hissed shut, and as the bus pulled away, Christopher threw his backpack on the snow and hunched over, scooping up snow and compacting it with his bare hands.

This was only going to escalate, Charlotte thought, watching them through the frosted window.

Christopher lobbed a snowball toward Sam who easily ducked it, his long dark hair swinging over his forehead.

Emily tossed one end of her red-and-white-checked scarf over her shoulder, pulled her books closer, and ran to the house. The soles of her brown leather boots were slippery, and she had a hard time finding purchase on the snow. From seemingly nowhere, another snowball sailed through the air but fell beside her on the ground.

Still clutching her books, she spun around to see where it had come from.

"No, fair, Uncle Pete," she yelled. "I don't have my mittens on."

Just beyond Emily, Charlotte could see her own son standing by the garage, his blue coveralls and yellow gloves streaked with grease.

He was laughing—and then a snowball caught him right on the chest.

The door of the porch swung open and Emily charged in, slamming it shut behind her.

"Those boys," she grumbled, but Charlotte could hear the edge of humor in her voice.

Charlotte walked to the porch to greet her granddaughter.

Emily was stamping the snow off her boots and brushing it off her coat. She glanced up and grinned at Charlotte. "If I'd had my mittens on, I'd have been able to fight back."

"And you'd probably be full of snow now," Charlotte said with a smile.

Emily slipped her coat off and gave it an extra shake as she shivered. "Those boys will be soaking wet when they come in." She gathered up her books and sniffed. "Boy, it smells good in here."

"I got an urge to do some Christmas baking. Want a cookie?"

"Sounds great."

"You better hurry before the boys come."

But no sooner had Charlotte spoken the words than the door slammed open again and Christopher, Sam, and Pete all came into the porch, laughing and pushing each other, snow falling off of them in clumps.

"You make sure you get rid of all that snow before you come into the house," Charlotte warned. "I just mopped the floor this morning."

Pete snapped off a salute, and Sam and Christopher laughed.

The phone rang again, and Charlotte felt another twinge of foreboding. Was it her prank caller?

For a moment she was tempted to let it ring, but then she pushed the thought aside and walked to the telephone.

"Charlotte? It's Anna." The breathless voice on the other end of the line sent Charlotte's heart pounding.

Her daughter-in-law had been on bed rest for several weeks to allay the complications of her pregnancy. Had something happened?

"Anna, are you okay?"

"This wasn't supposed to happen yet. Bill is still gone. I can't get hold of my mother. I don't have my suitcase packed. The girls are a mess—" Anna's voice was cut off by another gasp.

"Anna, what's wrong?"

"I think I'm in labor."

Chapter Two

"Grandma, I'm scared." Five-year-old Jennifer sniffed, wiping her nose with the sleeve of her shirt. Her dark hair hung in a tangle around her face, and her blue jeans had a rip in the knee. Who knows what the little girl had been doing before Anna left for the hospital? "I want my mama."

"I know, honey." Charlotte stroked the little girl's head and glanced at Bob, who was sitting across the hospital waiting room from her. Madison sat quietly beside him, her hands folded obediently in her lap, looking remarkably at ease for a seven-year-old. But Charlotte saw the pinched lines around her mouth. Madison was valiantly trying to be brave.

She could only imagine what might have gone through their minds while the girls waited for Bob and Charlotte to arrive.

Bob, never a fast driver, had been cautious on the snowy roads, and though it only took half an hour to get to Bill and Anna's place, Charlotte didn't relax until she saw Anna loaded on the ambulance and on her way to the hospital. After their previous scare with Anna's pregnancy, Charlotte didn't want to take any chances.

"What's taking so long?" Bob grumbled, pushing himself up from one of the hard chairs that hospitals seemed to favor. He strode over to the window overlooking the parking lot and glared past it to the houses festooned with twinkling Christmas lights.

"Jingle Bells" played softly over the hospital intercom, adding its festive notes to the tinsel and lights draped along the walls of the waiting room. Emily's cell phone, tucked in Charlotte's coat pocket, started to ring. She pulled it out, flipped it open, put it to her ear, and motioned for Jennifer to join her sister. "Hello?"

"Mom! Thank goodness I got through." It was Bill. "I called the farm, and Emily told me you had her cell phone. How's Anna?"

"She's in labor right now, but it's early yet. The doctor says the baby is stable and Anna is progressing nicely but she expects it will still be several hours before delivery. She's in good hands, Bill, and she and the baby are being closely monitored. Beyond that, she's in God's care."

"I'm stuck here in Chicago. It's snowing, and my flight is delayed. I won't be there for at least four hours, probably more." Bill's voice sounded heavy with regret and consternation. "I should be there. I should be with my wife. And what about my girls?"

Charlotte bit her lip as she glanced at Jennifer and Madison, still holding the candy canes a hospital volunteer had given them. "They're doing just fine, Bill. Don't worry about them."

"I should be there," he said again.

"Just come when you can. We'll take care of everything here."

"I'm so glad you're there, Mom. Anna's mom would be ordering the hospital staff around, fussing over Anna. Just like she did when the girls were born." Another sigh followed this.

"Like I said, you just relax. We'll take care of things here. Do you want to talk to the girls?"

"Thanks. That would be great."

Charlotte handed Madison the phone first. While the little girl talked to her father, Charlotte could see her visibly relax.

"Is that my daddy? Is he coming?" Jennifer sniffed and was about to wipe her nose again when Charlotte intervened, pulling a tissue out of her purse. "Use this, honey."

"Daddy wants to talk to Jennifer now." Madison handed the phone over, and Jennifer snatched it out of her hand.

"Are you coming, Daddy?" Jennifer asked, clutching the phone, her candy cane now lying on the floor. "Are you going to take care of Mommy, like she said? Why aren't you here right now? Can we go to the farm with Grandma and Grandpa if you don't come? I want to see Toby and the horses. Can I?"

Charlotte held her hand out. "Say good-bye to your daddy and then give me the phone," she said.

"But I'm not done talking to him," Jennifer pouted.

She never would be, Charlotte thought. Jennifer was a most loquacious young girl.

"You can talk to him later. I need to talk to him now."

Jennifer's expression turned mutinous, but she gave in and handed the phone to her grandmother. Under any other circumstances Charlotte might have gently reprimanded her, but today the girls' lives had just been thrown topsy-turvy. They had seen their mother in pain and were now sitting in a cold, unfamiliar hospital. It was understandable that they were out of sorts.

"We'll take care of everything, Bill. Just make sure you drive safely once you arrive, okay?"

"I'll come as soon as I can. Say hello to Anna for me."

Charlotte said good-bye and glanced at the girls, uncertain of what to do.

"Grandma," Madison said, "can we go to the farm?"

Charlotte was already regretting the decision to bring the girls to the hospital with their mom.

She stroked Jennifer's back and gave an encouraging smile to Madison as she picked up the discarded candy cane. "Can you girls just sit here a moment? I need to talk to your grandfather."

Jennifer sniffed again but used the tissue this time; Madison nodded.

Charlotte tossed the candy in the garbage and walked over to Bob, who stood by the window, his hands shoved in the pockets of his winter coat, his shoulders hunched as he stared outside. "Bill's not going to be here for a while. I'm wondering if you should take the girls back to the farm."

Bob glanced back at the girls, and then at Charlotte. "But what about Anna?"

"I'm staying here until Bill gets back. Pete can come and pick me up later on."

"But what if he's late?"

"Then I might have to find a place to stay for the night. I can take a cab to a hotel."

Charlotte could see the protest rising to Bob's lips, and she wondered what would bother him more: her being away from the farm or the cost of staying at a hotel overnight.

"I guess I'll take the girls back home. What about clothes for them?"

"I think I have some of their spare clothes in the hall closet. Emily can help you sort them out."

Bob pushed his fingers through his thinning hair and then gave Charlotte a weak smile. "I don't like leaving you here, but I don't like the idea of Anna being alone either."

Charlotte patted him on the shoulder, stood on tiptoe, and brushed a kiss over his grizzled cheek. "Thanks, Bob. I've got Emily's phone; I'll let you know how things are going."

The girls looked up when she came back, Jennifer swinging her legs, looking hopeful. "Are we going to the farm?"

She'd heard. Charlotte had forgotten how intent children could be when there was even the slightest hint they were the topic of a conversation.

"Yes, you are. And I'm staying with your mom."

Jennifer jumped off the chair, grabbed her winter coat, and slipped her arms in the sleeves as Charlotte spoke.

"But what about my daddy?" Madison said, her voice sounding small and afraid.

"He's coming. I'll wait for him here," Charlotte assured the little girl. She knelt down beside her, stroking her hair back from her face. "Your mommy and daddy would want to know that you girls are comfortable and safe at the farm, okay?"

"And we can play with Toby, remember?" Jennifer chimed in. "And us and Christopher can play hide-and-seek in the attic, and maybe we can go sledding and make a snow fort again."

Madison began to smile as her sister laid out the potential itinerary; and then she slipped off her chair and let Charlotte help her with her coat.

"And as soon as your little brother is born, I'll call and let you know." Charlotte zipped up Madison's coat.

She kissed the girls good-bye and watched as they followed Bob down the hall, their shoes squeaking on the shining floor. With a sigh, she turned back to the dog-eared three-month-old women's magazine she had been reading and was about to settle in for a long, boring wait when a voice interrupted.

"Mrs. Stevenson?" A young nurse wearing pink scrubs decorated with a Christmas wreath pin approached Charlotte with a tentative smile. "Are you Anna Stevenson's mother?"

"Mother-in-law." Charlotte put aside the magazine. "Is everything okay?"

"Everything's fine, but Anna is getting a little panicky. She said her husband was supposed to be her coach..." The nurse fluttered her hands as her brown eyes scanned the room. "I'm guessing he's not here yet?"

"He won't be for a few hours."

"*Hours?*" The word came out in a squeak of dismay.

Charlotte got up. "May I see her?"

"Please. Could you?" The nurse gave Charlotte a nervous smile and took a step back toward the room. "She's quite upset, and she won't settle down."

Charlotte wasn't surprised. Anna was a very intense young woman and could be demanding even when she was in a good mood. In pain and frightened—Charlotte could just imagine the scenario.

Anna was sitting up in the bed, tugging at her hospital gown, her cheeks flushed, her hair disheveled. "Can't you get me something that fits better than this hideous thing? I had a perfectly good nightgown to wear here..." Her voice trailed off as she realized Charlotte wasn't a nurse. "Oh, hello, Charlotte. Where're the girls?"

"Bob took them back to the farm. Bill just called. His plane is delayed."

Anna pressed one hand to her mouth, as if holding herself in. "He has to come. I didn't have the girls on my own. He needs to be here for his son. He needs to be here for me."

"I know he feels terrible, Anna, and he's coming as quickly as he can."

"I want him to be here. This is his son that's getting born." Anna's mouth drooped, and Charlotte suspected she was close to tears. She felt bad for her daughter-in-law, but the reality was, when Charlotte had gone through labor and delivery she'd been thankful Bob wasn't at her side.

She was about to leave when suddenly Anna arched her back, clenching her fists and reaching toward Charlotte. "Don't go!" she cried out. "I don't want to be alone. I can't do this alone."

Charlotte thought of the harried nurse who had brought her here and for a split second wondered if she really wanted to stay. Then she chided herself for her un-Christian attitude. Her daughter-in-law needed her. So she hurried back to Anna's side and gently grasped her arm. "Just lie back, Anna. Don't fight it."

"I just want them to give me some drugs. Why don't they just give me an epidural?"

Charlotte didn't know the answer to that question. She'd never had anything like that when she was having children. Right at that moment a young woman strode in wearing a lab coat with a stethoscope hanging out of one pocket, flipping through pages on a metal clipboard. Her name tag said Dr. Carson. She glanced at the board, then at Anna.

"How's Mom?"

"I'm in pain," Anna growled, clinging to Charlotte's arm, her manicured fingernails digging in. "I want an epidural."

The doctor shook her head. "I'm sorry, Anna. You know you're not far enough along in labor. We don't want it to wear off too soon. But when you're a little closer to delivery, I'll definitely order you one."

Anna tried to sit up, grimacing again, and Charlotte caught her by the arm. "Just relax, Anna. The more you fight it, the worse it becomes."

Dr. Carson shot a grateful glance Charlotte's way. "She's right, Anna," she said. "You'll have to breathe your way through this first part. And try to relax. You can do it. You've done it before." The doctor gave Anna a pat on the shoulder and then left.

"Try to relax. Is she kidding me?" Anna snarled, dropping her head back on the pillow. "Where is Bill? Why isn't he here?"

Charlotte poured Anna a cup of ice water and handed it to her. "Here. Would you like a drink?"

Anna took a few sips and then handed it back. "The girls are okay?"

"They're fine," Charlotte assured her. She glanced around the room, wondering how she could distract her daughter-in-law, but all she saw was Anna's coat thrown over the back of a chair and her shoes on the floor. "Where's your bag?"

To Charlotte's surprise, Anna's mouth trembled and a tear slipped out of one corner of her eye. "I didn't have time to pack one. I thought I had time to get ready. I was supposed to have a couple more weeks. I don't even have the baby's clothes here. And I had such a cute outfit for him."

In the confusion of getting Anna to the hospital,

Charlotte had forgotten to remind her to get her things together. "I'm sure we can get all of that to you before you come home."

"My mother knows where everything is. If she were home, she could just pop down to our house like she always does. What's the use of having a mother live so close by if she's not there when you need her?" Anna seemed to grow more agitated and breathed heavily as Charlotte tried to think of how to distract her.

Anna closed her eyes and another tear escaped. "I'm scared," she whispered. "This hurts way more than it did with the girls."

"Each pregnancy is different," Charlotte said, doubting the words soothed Anna but not knowing what else to say.

Anna sucked in a quick breath and arched her back again.

Charlotte stroked her arm. "Don't fight it. Loosen your shoulders. That's good. Now your hands. Breathe in really slowly and out really slowly. Now relax your feet and your legs." She pitched her voice low, and softened her tone, just like she had done when she put her children to bed all those years ago.

As she spoke, she saw Anna's fists unclench and felt relieved that she wasn't fighting as hard as she had been.

"I need to be distracted. Tell me about the kids. What are they up to?" Anna asked, breathing more normally. "Tell me about Sam, Emily, and Christopher. Has Sam figured out which college he wants to go to?"

"Sam is working on college application forms, though he seems to be dragging his feet on them. Emily is absorbed in fashion magazines, as always, and Christopher has taken up drawing."

"And Pete? Has he figured out where he and Dana are going to live?"

"I'm not sure. That's something they'll have to figure out together."

Anna drew in a quick breath through her nose, her gaze suddenly focused on the ceiling. "Here it comes again. This is a bad one. I can't believe they won't—" She gasped and clenched the bed rails.

Charlotte looked around the room for a book. Maybe reading to Anna would distract her. She opened the drawer of the side table and found a Bible nestled inside. "Do you want me to read to you?"

Anna nodded, her lips pressed together.

"Just make sure you keep your muscles loose when you feel the pain coming on," Charlotte said quietly. She opened the Bible to the Psalms and glanced over the pieces before she started.

"Let's start with a familiar one," she said, hooking her foot around the leg of a nearby chair and pulling it closer. She hoped the known cadences and rhythms would help soothe Anna. "Psalm 23," she read aloud. "The Lord is my shepherd; I shall not want. He makes me lie down in green pastures. He leads me beside still waters. He restores my soul."

As she read, Anna reached across the bed rail and clutched Charlotte's hand, and in the quiet of the hospital room, Charlotte felt a connection with her daughter-in-law she'd never experienced before.

"I've always liked that psalm," Anna said quietly when Charlotte finished. "The first time I heard it was at your house. I think Bob read it after supper. I thought that was so interesting."

Charlotte frowned. "Really? That was the first time you'd heard it?"

Anna shifted on the bed, wincing as she did so. "My mom and dad seldom went to church. I really didn't go regularly until I met Bill." She gave Charlotte a careful smile. "I started going more often because of him. I never told you that before."

"We never talked much about those things," Charlotte said carefully.

She and Anna had never been especially close. When Anna started dating Bill, she was so different from the country girls Bill had dated earlier; Charlotte had always felt a bit uncomfortable around her. Anna was always such a fashion plate and a bit aloof. And, truth be told, Anna had a difficult personality that made it hard to get truly close to her. She prided herself on her honesty, which often translated to being blunt and outspoken. She and Pete had never gotten along.

After she and Bill got married, they moved to River Bend, near Anna's mother. Anna naturally confided in her mother more than Charlotte, and when she did come to the farm, their visits were short.

And when Emily, Sam, and Christopher came, she initially saw them as rivals for Charlotte and Bob's attention.

Now Anna gave Charlotte a careful smile, which was quickly replaced by a another grimace and a tight squeezing of Charlotte's hand.

"OK," Charlotte said in a soothing tone. "Just breathe. S-l-o-w-l-y in . . . and slowly out. Slowly in and slowly out."

Anna followed her directions and Charlotte could see her visibly relax. She turned to Charlotte. "Can you read another psalm to me? The one about God being our dwelling place?"

Charlotte frowned as she paged through the Bible, trying to recall which one Anna meant.

"Bob read it one Christmas. There was something in there about generations," Anna said, stroking her mounded stomach. "And something about establishing the works of our hands?"

"Psalm 90," Charlotte remembered now. She flipped through the Bible, found it, and began reading, but decided on sharing only the first and last verses since they were the most soothing. While she read, she glanced over at Anna. A gentle smile played over her mouth, and her fingers rhythmically stroked her stomach, as if assuring the baby inside that all would be well.

As she read, on impulse, Charlotte reached over again and covered Anna's hand with her own, creating the connection through the generations that she'd been reading about in the Bible.

Her son's son was about to be born, she thought, hoping, praying that Bill would come on time to be there when it happened.

The next few hours slipped by as Charlotte alternately coached Anna through the labor and read to her. Talked to her and offered her ice chips when she needed them. And in that time they ceased to be mother-in-law and daughter-in-law; they were simply two women sharing the elemental bond of childbirth.

By the time the doctor came to administer the epidural, however, Anna was again struggling to stay on top of her pain with her breathing. Charlotte glanced at the clock one more time and sent up yet another prayer that Bill would come soon.

"You have to lie still," the doctor was saying to Anna, who lay on her side, facing Charlotte.

Charlotte held her hand and talked to her and she could see Anna relax.

Then, just as the doctor finished, a woman strode quickly into the room. Her height was enhanced by her gray hair, which was teased into an immaculate bouffant; her elegant bearing was accentuated by her tailored sage-green suit.

Anna's mother, Helen Adlai.

"Anna. Honey. I'm here." Mrs. Adlai gave Charlotte a polite smile, but in the presence of such immaculate elegance, Charlotte felt keenly aware of her faded blue jeans and the frayed edges of her everyday shirt. Unconsciously she put one hand to her hair, adjusting her bob, fiddling with the bobby pin that held it back from her face.

"I think I can take over now," Mrs. Adlai said, moving to the side of the bed where Charlotte sat. "You've been most helpful, Charlotte."

Charlotte relinquished her hold on Anna's hand and stepped aside and left the room to allow mother and daughter some time alone.

She felt suddenly superfluous, but at the same time, a sense of peace enveloped her. Being with Anna, helping her through this part of her labor, had been a precious experience, and she was thankful she had been there for her.

But now Anna's mother was here, and Charlotte felt sure Anna preferred having her mother at her side.

Charlotte pulled Emily's phone out of her pocket as she glanced at the clock in the waiting room. It was already 9:30, but it would take Pete only about half an hour to come get her. In spite of her brave words to Bob, she really had no desire to stay in a hotel overnight.

"Mom! Where is she? Where's Anna?"

Charlotte spun around in time to see a tall man rushing

toward her, his overcoat flowing out behind him, and she felt a pulse of thankfulness.

Bill.

She walked toward him and was, to her surprise, gathered in a hug. "I'm so glad you're here," he said, squeezing her tightly and then drawing away. "I feel so bad that I was gone."

"You couldn't have known," she assured him, brushing a bit of snow off his topcoat. "Anna's mother is with her now. You might want to collect yourself before you head in there."

Bill sank into the nearest chair and shoved his hand through his hair just as his father had done only a few hours ago. "I can't believe I was gone. I feel so bad."

"I'm sure once she sees you, all will be forgiven," Charlotte said with a smile.

"How did you get here?" he asked.

"Your father and I drove here together. I told him as soon as you came I would call Pete to come pick me up."

"Sure. That's great." Bill heaved a sigh, and then pushed himself to his feet, shooting anxious glances over his shoulder. "I should go see Anna. See how my wife and my son are doing."

"I was just about to phone Pete when you walked up." Bill gave her an absent pat on the shoulder and then hurried away to be at his wife's side.

Charlotte had to smile. When she'd had her children, Bob waited outside until the doctor came and told him it was over. Now, things were so much different. She couldn't decide which way she liked better.

Each had its own positives, she thought as she punched in the numbers for home.

She went downstairs to get a cup of coffee while she

waited, not wanting to be in the way. She got back just in time to meet Pete sauntering down the hall. He wore one of his favorite hats—a replica of a World War I flying ace, the flaps hanging down, untied—and a stained, down-filled jacket over the top of his loose blue jeans.

He brightened when he saw her. "Ready to go?"

"Pete. Good to see you." Bill came out of Anna's room just at that moment, still wearing his topcoat over his suit.

Charlotte had to smile at the vast difference between her two sons.

Bill addressed Charlotte. "Anna would like you to come in the room. I came out before but you were gone."

"I just went to get some coffee." Charlotte slipped her coat on, tiredness falling on her like a cloak. She hadn't realized how exhausted she was until now.

"Could you come just for a minute?" Bill asked.

Charlotte nodded as she buttoned up her coat, brushing at a stain and then laughing at herself. She was who she was. A woman who lived and worked on a farm. She had no need to feel ashamed of how she looked or dressed compared with Anna's mother.

"Pete, you want to come in?"

A look of sheer horror dropped over Pete's face, and Charlotte had to smile. He had watched untold births of calves and a number of foals and puppies, yet he blanched at the merest hint of human birth. He held his hands up, waving them dismissively. "No. I'm fine. I'll stay here and . . ."—he glanced down at Charlotte's half-full cup of coffee—". . . make sure no one takes Mom's coffee."

Bill frowned, but Charlotte fully understood Pete's reluctance. She took Bill's arm, and together they walked into the room.

Anna was sitting up, her hair brushed and, of all things, wearing lipstick. Her mother was buffing her nails. "You want to look good for the pictures afterward, honey. I have the video camera as well . . ."

"I don't think we'll be filming this, Mother Adlai."

Charlotte was pleased to hear the note of finality in Bill's voice.

"But it is such a miracle . . ."

"It will stay an unfilmed miracle." Bill brought Charlotte to the other side of Anna's bed. "My mom is leaving now. She wants to say good-bye."

Anna reached over with her free hand, a genuine smile lifting her lips. "Thanks for being with me," she said, squeezing Charlotte's hand. "I'm glad you stayed."

Charlotte stepped closer and gently brushed a strand of dark hair away from her face. "I am too. You look much more relaxed."

"The miracle of an epidural," she said but winced momentarily. "Not entirely foolproof, but much, much better."

"She's doing very well now that I'm here," Mrs. Adlai said with a polite smile.

"I'm sure she is," Charlotte said, patting Anna on the shoulder and realizing where her outspoken and blunt daughter-in-law got those tendencies.

Charlotte bent over and kissed Anna's forehead. "You take care, my dear. We'll be praying for you."

"Thanks." Anna squeezed Charlotte's hand just a bit tighter. "That means a lot to me."

"Anna, darling, you simply must take better care of these cuticles," Mrs. Adlai said suddenly.

Bill released a long-suffering sigh, and Charlotte felt a brush of pity for her oldest son. He might be bombastic at times and a bit full of himself, but he certainly had his hands full with these two.

"I'd like to pick up the girls tomorrow," Mrs. Adlai said. "Would it be possible to have them ready?"

Charlotte couldn't help a pang of dismay. She loved having all her grandchildren together. It didn't happen very often.

"I was hoping they could at least spend the day with us," she said.

"That won't be necessary."

Bill frowned, sensing his mother's disappointment. "Why don't you get them in the evening? The girls don't often get to spend a whole day with their cousins, and they love being on the farm."

"Mother might not have enough time then to go all the way to the farm," Anna said.

Charlotte felt a pang of disappointment when Anna took her mother's side. She shouldn't have been surprised, but at the same time she thought the moment they had shared would have made a bit of a difference.

"I'd like the girls to have some time with their cousins," Bill said firmly. "And I'd be willing to pick them up tomorrow evening."

Mrs. Adlai held Anna's gaze as if challenging her, and then lifted one shoulder in an elegant shrug. "Of course. I understand." She gave Charlotte another polite smile. "Thank you so much for taking care of the girls. It's much appreciated."

Charlotte simply smiled and was thankful when Bill ushered her out of the room. She didn't feel comfortable around Anna's mother.

"As soon as the baby is born, we'll call," Bill said.

"We'll be praying for Anna and the baby," Charlotte said, squeezing his arm.

"Thanks, Mom." He glanced over his shoulder and delivered a sigh. "I better get back in there before Anna's mother figures she should give Anna a pedicure as well."

Charlotte waved good-bye and as she and Pete left, she had to smile. *Like mother like daughter*, she thought. And yet, not. In the moments she and Anna had shared, something had shifted and changed for the better.

Please watch over her, Lord, she silently prayed as she and Pete drove back in the dark to the farm. *Please ease her pain and let them have a healthy child.*

The drive back to the farm was quiet. Charlotte was content to look at the Christmas lights of the town, and then, as they drove into the country, to see how other people had decorated their houses.

Christmas was such a festive occasion and now, with another grandchild on the way, Charlotte felt richly blessed and wonderfully satisfied.

Joy to the world, she thought as they drove along.

Half an hour later, Pete turned the truck onto their driveway, and the twin cones of light from his headlights swept over familiar landscape. He stopped in front of the house, and Charlotte made a mental note to ask Bob to put up their own Christmas lights.

Golden rectangles of light spilled from the lower floor of the house onto the snow, and inside, Charlotte saw Bob's stooped figure bending over to look out the window. He was joined by Christopher, and then Emily.

They'd been waiting, she thought as a blessed sense of well-being settled over her.

Her family had been waiting for her to come home.

Chapter Three

What was a fire engine doing in their bedroom?

Charlotte dragged open her eyes, blinking in the half-light filtering into the bedroom, her heart pounding as that horrible sound cut into the silence of the early morning.

The noise sounded again, and Charlotte finally realized it was the handset of the cordless telephone she had taken to bed last night.

She pounced on it, fumbling as she tried to find the button that would answer the call.

"Bill?" she said when she finally made the connection.

"Hello, Mom. Just wanted to let you know that Anna had the baby an hour ago, at four o'clock. A baby boy, just like we expected—seven pounds, six ounces. His name is Will—Will Robert Stevenson."

Charlotte lay back in the bed, smiling into the morning. *A new grandson. Will Robert Stevenson.* She tried out the name of her newest family member. "Congratulations, Bill. What a blessing from the Lord."

"That's for sure." Bill sighed.

"You sound tired."

"I'm beat. Anna was a trouper, but she had a lot of hemorrhaging so the doctor wants to keep an eye on her, probably until Monday."

Charlotte's heart started up again. "Is she okay?"

"She's very tired but still insists she can come home tomorrow. She already had an argument with the doctor over that this morning."

Charlotte had to smile, thinking of her daughter-in-law being determined to do what she wanted to do.

"But Anna staying another day means you might have the girls an extra day, if that's okay," Bill asked.

"Of course, my dear," Charlotte said. "I'll gladly keep the girls."

"Anna is absolutely beat. They needed to give her a transfusion so I was wondering if you could wait and bring the girls to come see her tomorrow. She really needs her rest."

"Of course. That's not a problem."

"I already told Mom Adlai, so neither of us will be coming to pick up the girls tonight."

"And how is the baby?"

"Apparently his bilirubin levels are a bit high, so they're going to do something called phototherapy with him." Bill sighed again. "Things went so smoothly with Madison and Jennifer. This pregnancy seems to have been nothing but complications."

"Jaundice is not uncommon," Charlotte assured Bill. "And Anna is in good hands in the hospital. You don't need to worry."

She heard Bill's sigh across the phone line and sent up a quick prayer for him.

"I'm trying not to, but it's pretty hard seeing your wife in such distress and the baby having a problem too."

"We'll be praying for you," Charlotte said.

"I knew you'd say that," Bill said. "Anyway, can you tell Dad and Pete and the girls? Tell them I'll call again this afternoon sometime with an update."

"I will."

"I hope the girls are okay with all of this."

"I'm sure they will be," Charlotte said. "We'll keep them occupied. Now make sure you get some rest. You must be exhausted yourself."

"Yeah. I am kind of bushed." He paused, and Charlotte sensed he was yawning. "I'll keep you posted if I have more news."

Charlotte said good-bye and then lay back in bed, holding the phone close, as if keeping the news to herself for a few more moments.

Thank You, Lord, she breathed. *Thank You that so far things are well. Please be with Anna and the baby. Grant them both healing.*

Then she gave her husband's shoulder a gentle shake to tell him the wonderful news. When he heard, he simply smiled and rolled over to catch a bit more sleep.

Charlotte debated waiting to tell the girls, but when she heard giggles coming from Emily's room upstairs, she knew they were already awake. So she climbed the stairs and knocked lightly on the door and then went in.

As she had suspected, they were both sitting up in their sleeping bags, looking at her with expectant faces. Emily slept soundly on her own bed.

"That was my daddy on the phone, wasn't it?" Jennifer said, getting to her knees and grinning at Charlotte. "My little brother is born, isn't he?"

"*Our* little brother," Madison corrected.

Charlotte smiled at the two girls, putting her finger to her lips so they wouldn't wake the other children. "Yes. Your little brother is born," she whispered. "His name is Will Robert Stevenson. And he weighed seven pounds and six ounces."

"Yay! A little brother," Jennifer cried out, bouncing on her sleeping bag.

"Ssssh. You don't want to wake up Emily and Sam," Madison warned, whispering as though she enjoyed having a secret. "Can we go see my mommy?" she asked.

Charlotte sat down on the floor with them and gave Madison a quick hug. "Not today. Your mommy is very tired and needs a lot of rest. We'll go tomorrow. After church."

"That means we can stay here another day," Jennifer said. "Yay!"

Charlotte put her finger to her lips again, and Jennifer clapped her hand over her mouth. But Charlotte could see her eyes sparkling above her fingers. "Yay," she whispered.

"I can't wait to see my little brother," Madison whispered, settling back into her sleeping bag. She gave a light yawn, as Charlotte pulled the top of the bag up around her shoulders.

"You girls try to get some more sleep. When you wake up, we'll do some baking, okay?"

"Gingerbread men? For Christmas?" Jennifer asked, still sitting on her knees.

"Yes. And we can make some extra ones for your mother." Charlotte kissed her granddaughter's forehead and eased Jennifer back into her sleeping bag. "Now try to get some sleep."

The girls obediently rolled over onto their sides, but as Charlotte closed the door, she could hear Jennifer whispering to her sister, making plans for their unexpected extra day at the farm.

She went downstairs and crawled back into bed, hoping to catch a bit more sleep herself, but she kept thinking about little Will and wondering what he looked like. She'd find out soon enough, she thought, rolling over onto her side as well.

Just before sleep reclaimed her, she sent up another prayer for the newest member of the Stevenson family and that all would be well with Anna.

"WHAT DO YOU NEED NOW?" Christopher asked, hanging over the engine that his Uncle Pete was working on.

Christopher had already had his breakfast, and he didn't have to help with the dishes, and now Madison, Emily and Jennifer were making cookies and didn't need his help. Besides, he didn't want to listen to Jennifer and Madison talking on and on about their little brother. He wanted to help his Uncle Pete.

"A three-fourths socket," Pete grunted.

"I can get it," Christopher said. "Just tell me where it is."

"Top drawer of the tool chest."

Christopher nodded as he scurried off to the chest, opened a drawer, and then frowned. He had no idea what a three-fourths socket looked like.

"Which one would it be?"

"It would have a three and a four on it—three-fourths," Uncle Pete said.

Christopher looked and looked but couldn't find it.

Suddenly Uncle Pete reached past him and easily found the one he wanted.

"How do you know which one it is?" Christopher asked, following Uncle Pete back to the snowmobile he was trying to fix up.

"Smart like a fox," Uncle Pete said as he fitted the socket on the end of the wrench and dived once more into the innards of the snowmobile he had brought home yesterday.

It was early Saturday morning, and Christopher was very excited. His Uncle Pete had promised him the first ride when the snowmobile was fixed. Christopher picked up a screwdriver his uncle had dropped on the floor. He set the handle on the palm of his hand and tried to balance it. "Why didn't you find a machine that worked?"

"I bought this one because it was a great deal."

"But you might not get it working."

"Inconceivable," Uncle Pete declared with a grin. "I'll get it working in just a couple of hours."

Christopher toyed with the screwdriver, his head full of pictures of Uncle Pete driving the snowmobile all over the snow-covered pasture, pulling him, Jennifer, and Madison on the big tire tube Pete had gotten from his friend Brad. Pictures that he'd had in his head ever since he saw the photo of the snowmobile on the counter at AA Tractor Supply. Christopher had gotten tired of waiting in the truck for his uncle, so he'd gone inside and found Uncle Pete and Brad Weber talking about how much Uncle Pete should pay for it.

As soon as Uncle Pete had seen Christopher he'd pulled the paper off the counter and shoved it into the back pocket of his blue jeans. Then he'd told Christopher it was their secret and that he wasn't supposed to tell anyone.

"How long will it take?" Christopher asked now, putting the screwdriver back on the floor.

"Only a few more hours." Uncle Pete looked up at him, a smear of grease on his nose and his cheek. "Are you bored? Do you want to go in the house and hang out with your cousins?"

Christopher shrugged. "Not really. Grandma's making gingerbread cookies with them, and I thought I could help you."

But all he'd done so far was hand Uncle Pete a rag and watch him work. He didn't feel like he was much help to his uncle at all.

"Pretty cool about your new little cousin, right?"

Christopher nodded. Grandma had been so excited all morning. Except she kept looking at the clock, like she was expecting Uncle Bill to call her again.

"Okay, this is about done," Uncle Pete said with a grunt. "Just need to get the spark plugs cleaned up and the carb working, and we'll be in business."

He pushed himself away from the vehicle and headed toward the tool chest.

"I can get what you need," Christopher volunteered.

"S'okay. It's easier if I just get it myself. I want to get this thing done as quickly as possible," Uncle Pete said, waving a greasy hand toward Christopher. "Ah, here it is, just where I left it last." Uncle Pete picked up a screwdriver from the floor beside the chest.

"Aren't you supposed to put your tools away when you're done with them?" Christopher asked, following his uncle back to the machine.

"You sound like Grandpa now," Uncle Pete said, fitting the screwdriver onto something in the engine. "Next thing you know you'll be asking me what I'm doing about a place to live after me and Dana get married."

Christopher squatted down to watch Uncle Pete work. "You can't move Miss Simons into your old place. It's all smoky and dirty from the fire."

It had been exciting and scary when they'd had a fire in the tractor shed last month. Christopher still felt bad about it, even though the insurance man had said it wasn't his lightning-rod experiment that had caused the fire. But now Uncle Pete and Miss Simons couldn't live there, and Uncle Pete had to come up with something else. For now he was staying in the spare bedroom, but he couldn't stay there forever.

"You're not telling me anything I don't already know," Uncle Pete said. He sounded a bit grumpy. "I've got enough to think about just getting the tractor shed replaced and trying to figure out how to pay for . . ." He stopped talking and gave the screw he was tightening an angry twist.

"Pay for what? Sam's college and the house?"

Uncle Pete pushed his cap back with the back of his hand and gave Christopher a funny smile. "You know you're like a little vacuum cleaner, sneaking around the farm, sucking up bits and pieces of conversation and storing them away."

Christopher wasn't sure if that was a good thing or not. "But I'm right, aren't I? The farm won't have enough money to pay for Sam's education and your house, will it?"

Uncle Pete tapped Christopher on the end of the nose with his screwdriver. "You don't need to get fussed about that, buddy. The farm is doing just fine."

Christopher grinned at his uncle, but at the same time, he knew that Grandma and Grandpa were a bit worried. He'd heard them one night when he couldn't sleep and they were talking downstairs in the family room.

"But you still need a place to live," Christopher said, knowing that sometimes, like Grandpa said, Pete had to learn to stay on task.

"Yeah. I suppose. I just don't have the energy right now to come up with a house plan."

"I could help you."

Uncle Pete gave him a funny look. "How?"

Christopher straightened and tapped his finger on his chin. "I could go on the Internet. Get some ideas. Draw up a plan myself."

Uncle Pete pulled on what Christopher considered his thinking face. "Okay. That would give you something to do. Maybe you could go work on that right now."

Christopher frowned. "No. I have to help you get the snowmobile going first."

"Right," Uncle Pete said, wiping his hand on a rag. "Of course."

"You said you wanted to get it going by lunchtime—in time to get a Christmas tree," Christopher reminded him, excited to think about picking out a tree. Because once they got a tree, that would mean Christmas was really coming.

"Did you pick one out yet?"

"Grandpa said he found one this year." Christopher was a little bit disappointed about that. Last year he'd spent a lot of time looking for exactly the right tree. He was going to do that again this year, but Grandpa came home one day and said he knew exactly where they could get their tree this year. Oh well. That didn't matter. It was more important that they get a tree, Christopher reminded himself as he bent over to help Uncle Pete finish on time.

Or actually, watch Uncle Pete finish on time.

Chapter Four

"You don't think I should get Arielle a ring for Christmas?" Sam switched the phone to his other ear as he slouched against the headboard of his bed.

"You want to start planning a wedding, dude?" Jake's incredulous voice told Sam everything he needed to know.

"Okay. Okay. Dumb suggestion. I thought all girls liked jewelry." Sam sighed, fiddling with a loose thread on the hem of his blue jeans. In a way that was a relief. He'd set some money aside for her Christmas present, but the list of other things he had to buy got bigger every day.

Another pair of blue jeans, a fan belt for his car, and he also had picked Grandpa's name for Christmas and had zip, zero, and zilch clue what to get him. "So a ring is too much, but flowers are lame," he continued. "You're no help, man."

"Gift cards are easy."

"That's like saying, 'Oh, yeah, I needed to get you a present but didn't feel like thinking much about it.' That's a guaranteed one-way street to being single again."

"Hey, I just advise."

"I guess I'll think of something." A sudden knock on the door caught his attention.

"Sam, are you using the phone?" Grandma's voice was muffled by the closed door. "I thought I asked everyone to keep it free. I'm waiting to hear more news from Bill about Anna."

Sam felt a jolt of guilt. He'd forgotten about Anna and the baby, his new cousin. Apparently there had been a few problems, and Grandma was a bit stressed about it all. "Hey, Jake, gotta go. Talk to you later, man." Sam hit the END button and then pushed himself off the bed.

Grandma stood by the door, her arms folded over her faded pink apron. Her lips were pressed together, and she was frowning. This was not looking good.

"Sorry, Grandma. I forgot." He handed Grandma the phone with an apologetic grin and was about to retreat back into his room when Grandma put her hand on the door. He figured she hadn't tracked him down just for the phone, but he could live in hope.

"There's something else you've forgotten," she said in that tone of voice that Sam knew better than to ignore. "There are a couple of packages of paper downstairs."

Sam knew exactly where she was going. "Well, I've been kind of busy with school and trying to get my car going. And soccer just ended, and that was taking up a lot of my time."

Grandma sighed one of those long, slow sighs that meant he had messed up. Again. "Sam, you need to get those application forms filled out and sent away by the end of the month."

"I've got time."

"You've had months. You're running out of time and excuses."

"I said I would." He didn't mean for that snotty edge to get into his voice, but he felt guilty. Which made him feel like he had to defend himself.

Grandma's lips got even tighter, and he knew he'd stepped over the line.

"Sorry, Grandma. I'm just feeling a bit pinched for time." *And money*, he added silently. "Besides, I thought I could apply online."

"I'm sure you did. But this way you have a chance to have someone look them over before you send them out. And this way, I can keep an eye on you better." Grandma added a quick smile to show she was teasing, but Sam could see from the snap in her eye that she kind of wasn't. "So I'm helping you out. I'd like you to come downstairs and work on them right now. The sooner you get them done, the better you'll feel. I don't want you to miss this opportunity."

Sam wasn't so sure about that. Because, the trouble was, lately Sam wasn't sure about much. Lately he felt as if his life had hit some kind of weird place with all kinds of possibilities ahead of him. And he just didn't know which one to pick.

He wasn't sure if he wanted to go to school, but he wasn't sure if he wanted to stay in Bedford. He felt like he wanted to move back to San Diego, but he had friends here.

Grandma didn't seem to care about any of that. She had already turned around and from the way she marched down the stairs, he knew he had to follow.

Downstairs, in the kitchen, it was chaos. Emily had the radio on some lame country station. Madison and Jennifer were trying to sing along. The kitchen counter was full of baking stuff, and it looked like they were making gingerbread cookies.

"You can do some practice answers on this," Grandma said, setting out a pad of paper on one corner of the kitchen table. "And here are the forms." She dropped the large heavy envelope, the one he'd been avoiding, on the table. Then she patted Sam on the shoulder, though she had to reach up to do it. "So, just get down and do it. You'll be glad you did."

Sam scratched his head and sighed. He doubted it, but he would be happy if everyone stopped nagging him about these dumb applications. So maybe if he got them done, the nagging would stop.

And once he was done, he was heading out to work on his car.

Half an hour later, Sam had managed to fill in his name, his address and phone number. He had stalled when he got to the part that asked his parents' marital status, his pencil hovering above the page.

Now that his mother was dead, did his dad have any legal rights?

Were Grandma and Grandpa really his legal guardians? He remembered when they went to that lawyer in Harding a couple of months ago, but they never told him or Emily what happened. Only that someday they would have to decide what they wanted to do about their father.

So was his dad still legally his dad?

Would Sam have to contact him about these application forms? Would Grandma and Grandpa be able to fill them out?

And where was his dad anyway? Last year Sam had tried to hunt him down, and when he was unsuccessful, he had tried to put the idea of finding his father behind him. But it seemed that no matter how hard he tried to forget his dad, the guy came up again and again.

Like a ghost.

He pulled another piece of paper out of the pile: APPLICATION FOR FEDERAL STUDENT AID.

Well, he'd certainly need some aid. He had precious little money in his account, and he was pretty sure he wouldn't be getting much from the farm.

A shriek broke into his tangled thoughts, and he jumped.

"No, Emily! You can't do that," Jennifer called out.

Sam sighed and picked up the paper again, trying to concentrate, but he couldn't. It was too noisy in here; that was all. He turned over a page on the pad of paper and started writing out some ideas for a present for Arielle.

Grandma hustled past the table toward the family room and shot him a quick glance. With a guilty start, he turned back to the forms.

Then the whine of the vacuum cleaner cut through the noise coming from the kitchen on the other side of him. Why did Grandma have to start cleaning now? Ever since he came downstairs she'd been fussing around the house, doing all kinds of useless cleaning and tidying. Like she couldn't sit still. As far as he knew, all that was wrong with Will was that he was jaundiced, whatever that was, and Aunt Anna was only tired. But Grandma seemed a bit stressed about it all.

"Emily, you're supposed to give the gingerbread man a happy face," Jennifer said with a laugh.

"This gingerbread man is seriously depressed." Emily pulled a sad face. "He just found out that the girl he wanted to be friends with on Facebook didn't want to be friends with him."

"What's Facebook?" Jennifer asked just as the phone began to ring. "And why doesn't she want to be friends with him?"

"Grandma always says you should try to be friends with everyone," Madison added in that annoying little whine that could cut right through your head. "It's the right thing to do."

Emily started snapping her fingers, making weird dance moves. "Everyone should be my friend," she chanted in time to her own beat. "It would be the living end."

Sam stuck his fingers in his ears, but he couldn't stop the crazy noise.

And then of course the phone was ringing.

Grandma hurried past him and snatched the phone off the cradle.

"Can I go up to my room, Grandma?" Sam asked as she said hello. "I can't concentrate here."

She held her hand up to him and shook her head as she listened. Then she frowned and talked a bit more. She sounded a bit worried, and against his will, Sam was intrigued.

"I'm sure the doctor knows what she's doing, Bill," Grandma was saying. "Make sure Anna listens to her. If she tries to move too much she could cause more problems." Grandma was quiet for a moment, and then she gave a funny smile. "Well, tell Mrs. Adlai to tell her. I'm sure Anna will listen to her mother, and tell her the girls can stay here as long as necessary. And yes, we'll all come after church tomorrow."

Sam groaned inwardly. He wanted to go to Jake's place after church tomorrow, but he figured Grandma and Grandpa wouldn't let him go unless he had these dumb forms filled out.

And that wasn't going to happen with those squealing girls around all day and night.

"Say hello to Anna for us," Grandma was saying. "And make sure she gets some rest."

She talked a bit more, hung up the phone, and then

turned to Jennifer and Madison, who were watching her like little mice.

"Are we going to see my mommy?" Jennifer said.

Grandma shook her head. "Sorry, honey, remember what I said? Your mommy is tired and needs her rest. We'll go see her tomorrow."

"But I want to see my mommy!" Jennifer whined. "And my little brother. Now."

Grandma sighed, and Sam guessed the girls needed a distraction. So did he.

"You know what I think would be cool?" Sam said, getting up from the table and leaving the dreaded forms behind. "We could go sledding."

"I want..." Jennifer stopped, mid-rant, and then sniffed. "Sledding?"

"When Grandpa cleared the snow off the yard, he pushed a hill up by the barn. I'll go get the sleds," Sam said, ducking into the porch before Grandma could protest.

He heard the excited chatter of the girls behind him as he pulled on his coat and hat and stuffed his feet into his boots. They stored sleds in the small toolshed, and as he started dragging them toward the house, he heard the buzz of a two-stroke engine.

Chain saw?

No. Too loud for that.

He stopped to listen as the noise grew louder. He turned and stared.

A snowmobile? Coming across the pasture? Who in the world...

Then, as the machine came closer and the noise grew louder, he started laughing. Pete was perched in the front, leaning over the handlebars, the flaps of his aviator hat flying in the wind. Christopher hung on behind him, laughing, his cheeks beet red from the wind and the cold. Snow spat up behind them from the spinning track.

Toby streaked behind them, her body low to the ground, her legs eating up the distance between her and the noisy machine. Pete pulled the snowmobile up beside Sam and cut the engine. "So. What do you think?"

"This was our surprise," Christopher shouted, his eyes bright, a grin splitting his face. "Me and Uncle Pete worked on it all morning. Well, Uncle Pete did most of the work. I kind of watched."

Sam didn't know what to say. Jake had a snowmobile, and he and Paul had a blast getting pulled around behind it on their snowboards. He never, ever thought in all his weirdest and wildest dreams that they would have one here.

"This is awesome!" He walked around the machine to have a closer look. It was an older model, and it probably didn't go as fast as the grasshopper-looking machine Jake had, but it was a snowmobile. And it could still pull.

"Yeah. Get the kids. We're going to burn a few doughnuts in the field and then, when we come back, we'll get the Christmas tree."

"Shouldn't we wait for Grandpa to finish up his chores?" Sam asked. "He was the one who knew where the Christmas tree was."

"I don't know if he'll go behind this thing," Pete snorted, wiping his nose with a bright red handkerchief. "But Mom might. And she probably knows where it is."

Sam followed them to the house at a jog, dragging the sleds behind him, Toby trotting behind him, her tongue hanging out of her mouth.

Christopher bailed off the snowmobile even before Pete

brought it to a full stop by the house. Sam caught up to him just as his little brother burst into the porch, spilling the good news.

"We're making doughnuts. On the snowmobile," he announced, mixing up Uncle Pete's words.

"What are you talking about?" Emily asked, zipping up Jennifer's jacket. Then she handed the little girl her mittens. "Here, Jennifer, put these on."

"Uncle Pete fixed up an old snowmobile," Sam said, still laughing at the idea. Way cool. He could hardly wait to tell his friends at school. "Uncle Pete wants to pull us around on it in the field."

"Snowmobile?" Grandma looked puzzled. She grabbed a coat and stepped outside. Sam could see her shake her head, but she was smiling.

"Uncle Pete is going to pull us behind the snowmobile on sleds," Sam said, zipping up his coat as he ran back outside to help Uncle Pete tie the sleds to the back of the machine.

But though the machine was still running, Uncle Pete was gone. Sam was about to go to the toolshed to get some rope when he saw Pete rolling a huge black inner tube across the yard. It was almost as tall as he was.

"We'll use this tube from the tractor tire," Pete was saying. "Way more fun."

The girls and Christopher spilled out of the house, and even Grandma came out, all bundled up. While she helped them figure out how they would all fit in the giant inner tube, Toby ran around them, eager to play again.

Grandma made Sam and Emily lie down across the tube first, their legs hanging over one side of the tube and their backs resting on the other side. Then she had the little girls sit down on top of them.

"Now, you make sure you hang on to each other. And Pete, you don't go too fast now," Grandma warned once everyone was in place.

Uncle Pete revved the engine, as if to tease Grandma. Christopher got on the snowmobile behind Uncle Pete. He leaned sideways to help turn the machine around, like Sam had seen Jake do, and then they were off down the driveway toward the open pasture. Snow spit out from behind them and sprayed over the tube riders as they bounced along over the snow, but they were all laughing so hard it didn't matter.

Sam tried to look behind to see if Toby was following, but he couldn't turn his head.

Then Pete swung them around, and the inner tube went faster and faster as it slid across the snow. Emily, Jennifer, and Madison were screaming, but Sam didn't care.

He was having a blast. Maybe Uncle Pete would let him drive it.

They came burning back into the yard, spun around in front of the house, and then slowed down. A truck was coming into the yard.

It was jacked up high off the ground, and the sun glinted off the shiny red paint job. Flashy unit, Sam thought. Probably some oil-field dude who'd gotten lost on his way to work.

The truck came to a stop, skidding a bit as it did so. As they whizzed past it, Pete waved, and Sam turned his head to get a better look at the fancy rig. He caught a glimpse of the driver.

And felt a frightening jolt of recognition.

Chapter Five

Charlotte had been watching the kids have a ball when she spotted the bright red truck coming down the driveway.

Puzzled, she walked toward the fancy vehicle as it parked. The sun shone off the windshield so she couldn't see who was driving. And then the driver climbed out.

"Hey, Charlotte," the man called out with a jaunty wave.

Charlotte stared. As recognition dawned, she felt as if someone had taken one of the icicles hanging from her roof and shoved it into her heart.

Kevin Slater.

The man no one had heard from in years.

Kevin Slater. Sam, Emily, and Christopher's father.

Seconds ticked by in her mind as she and Kevin stared at each other across the yard. Seconds that only a moment ago were benign and friendly, now felt weighted with merciless worry and fear.

What was Kevin doing back here?

What did he want, after all this time?

Her heart thumped so heavily in her chest, Charlotte thought it might jump completely free of her body.

Bob emerged from behind the barn and looked as surprised as Charlotte when he saw Kevin.

Kevin, however, didn't seem concerned in the least. He bounded up the walk full of good cheer and exuding confidence. His hair, once long and curly, was clipped short. His face, once so young looking, now seemed longer, leaner. He wore a hip-length leather coat, blue jeans, and cowboy boots.

He walked toward Charlotte, holding out his hand. "Good to see you again, Charlotte."

Good to see you again?

Were those inane words the only ones he could utter after everything that had happened?

All the events of the past two years crowded into her mind as her daughter's husband, her grandchildren's father, stood in front of her, his smile wide, guileless, his blue eyes bright, clear, and seemingly free of the shadows that had hovered over Charlotte's family the past two years.

"Why are you here?" The words came out sharper than she had intended. Harsher. But how could she temper them when this man had caused so much upheaval by disappearing, abandoning his family? When so many horrible things had happened since he left?

Kevin blinked his confusion as he lowered his still-outstretched hand and glanced toward Bob, as if looking for support. By this time the kids had climbed out of the tube and were making their way toward Charlotte, Bob, and Kevin.

Charlotte clamped down on her own panic and struggled to put her emotions in the right place.

Please, Lord. Help us through this moment. Please, Lord... But then her prayers faltered. She didn't even know what to pray for.

As Emily helped brush snow off Madison and Jennifer, Sam strode toward Kevin, who was now turning to face his elder son. Toby ran ahead of Sam, barking at the unknown man. It wasn't a bark of welcome. It was a bark of warning. Charlotte shushed the dog, who sidled up to her, the fur on the back of her neck raised.

But Kevin's attention was on his son.

"Sam? Is that you, son?" Kevin asked, his voice incredulous.

Charlotte continued to pray inarticulate prayers for Sam, for the other children, and for herself as she tangled her fingers in Toby's damp fur.

Please Lord, help the kids through this. Please, Lord. Help me through this.

Sam tugged his snow-encrusted stocking cap off his head and ran his hand through the disarranged strands. He nodded, his eyes narrow and wary. "Dad?"

Charlotte straightened and hugged herself against a sudden chill as Kevin nodded.

Sam angled his head to one side, as if to examine him further just as Emily, Christopher, and the two girls joined them.

"That was so cool," Emily was saying. "Sam, are you going to..." Her voice faded away as she glanced from Sam to Kevin.

Emily's eyes narrowed, her lips thinned, and she straightened, still holding Jennifer's and Madison's hands.

"What are you doing here?" Her question echoed Charlotte's, cutting through the heavy silence, accusing and angry.

"I'm here to visit you." Kevin granted her a lazy smile. "Can't a dad come and see his own kids?"

Emily strode past him, pulling Jennifer and Madison in her wake. "C'mon, girls, we have to finish decorating those gingerbread men."

Christopher sidled up to Sam, also looking up at his father. Kevin crouched down, his leather coat creaking in the cold. "So, this is my little Chrispeter."

"My name is Christopher," the boy corrected him, his voice sounding small and disoriented.

"Yeah. I know, but when you were born, Emily couldn't pronounce your name and called you Chrispeter instead."

"Mom never told me that," Christopher replied.

"Well, she probably didn't remember." Kevin smiled at his younger son and reached over to squeeze his arm. "Wow. Feel those muscles! I bet you're really strong."

Charlotte saw the beginnings of a smile tease one corner of Christopher's mouth. "I can be."

"You're probably a big help on the farm. I could use a big guy like you helping me at my work."

The smile blossomed, and Charlotte tried not to resent how smoothly Kevin had insinuated himself into this impressionable boy's life.

And thus was Denise seduced, she thought.

Kevin straightened just as Pete joined them, slapping the snow off his own hat. He too looked from Kevin to Sam and then to Charlotte.

Sam had his hand on his little brother's shoulder, as if protecting him. But Christopher had eyes only for Kevin.

"So. Here you are," Pete said, jutting his chin Kevin's way.

Definitely defensive, Charlotte thought, still wondering how they would navigate this minefield.

Pete had never cared for Kevin, and he'd thought even less of him when Denise ran away to marry him.

"Why're you here now?" Sam asked.

Sam's voice was cold, lifeless, and Charlotte didn't know what to make of his reaction. After all the work and turmoil Sam had endured last year to go looking for his father, she might have expected him to be overjoyed. In fact, she'd feared he would be. Feared he would want to immediately join his father and leave Bedford and his grandparents behind.

"Why are you here at all?" Pete snorted, and as his eyes narrowed, Charlotte knew she had to intervene or things might get ugly.

"Why don't we all go inside and have a cup of coffee?" she suggested, trying to sound more positive than she felt.

Kevin glanced back at her, his expression grateful. "Sure. That would be great."

The atmosphere on the porch was subdued as boots were kicked off and set on the plastic mats, snow brushed off coats and hung up, mittens laid out to dry.

Charlotte walked directly into the kitchen and pulled the coffeepot off the machine to fill it with water. "Can you get me the coffee out of the pantry?" she asked Emily. "Madison, can you get me a new filter from the drawer? It's the second one from the left. By the stove."

"Can I do something for our company, Grandma?" Jennifer piped in. "I'm a good helper."

Charlotte gave her a quick smile, thankful for the diversion of the two girls. "You can put cups on the table for me." She took the filter from Madison, the coffee from Emily, and then asked the girls to make up a plate of cookies.

"Can I do something, Grandma?" Christopher asked.

"That's okay, honey, you can sit down with... your father." It was surprisingly difficult to get those two words out. Charlotte turned to her oldest granddaughter. "Emily, can you make some hot chocolate?"

Emily worked in silence, shooting puzzled glances across the kitchen toward the table, where Kevin sat down beside Christopher. It was as if she wasn't sure herself what to make of her father.

Meanwhile, Charlotte silently made busy work for herself at the counter, waiting for the coffee to brew.

Kevin.

For years, the name had conjured up a vague and shadowy figure. Yes, the person in her mind had the blond hair and blue eyes this man in front of her had, but in Charlotte's imagination Kevin had stayed an ephemeral figure whose threat had dissipated with each passing month.

And now here he was, very real and very alive, pulling a chair up to their kitchen table, asking Pete about the farm as if he had never dropped out of everyone's lives all those years ago. As if he hadn't broken her daughter's heart and abandoned her and their children.

Pete's replies to Kevin's questions were terse, monosyllabic. Bob leaned back in his chair, his arms folded over his chest, watching Kevin suspiciously.

"Do you still farm the land?" Kevin was asking, still trying to get the conversation going.

Pete simply nodded.

"And still have cows?"

Another nod.

"We have horses too," Christopher piped up. "I did a report on them. Uncle Pete and Grandpa helped me. And I made a rocket for school too. And we had a food drive, and I helped our class win. And last year I was in the Christmas pageant, and so was Emily. And Sam has a girlfriend and Uncle Pete is going to get married and Emily knows how to sew now and she made a really pretty dress." He sounded pathetically eager to bring his father up to date on all the happenings in their lives.

Charlotte couldn't help noticing that everything he told Kevin had taken place on the farm. Christopher never once mentioned San Diego.

Or his mother.

Sam hovered between the kitchen and the family room as if uncertain of his place in this new upheaval in his life.

When Christopher finally finished his chattering, Kevin asked Pete a few more questions and then he apparently ran out of topics—or else he picked up on the awkwardness in the house, because he said nothing more.

"I have a cat. Named Lightning," Christopher offered.

"I don't think . . . he wants to hear about every little thing, buddy," Sam said, an edge of anger in his voice.

Christopher looked chastened, and Charlotte felt a moment's pity for him. He was so obviously trying to ease the awkwardness. Or, alternately, trying to win his father's approval.

In the ensuing quiet, the clock in the family room marked off the seconds, each tick sounding as loud as a gunshot. Kevin tapped his fingers on the table and then granted Madison a quick smile when she put a cup in front of him.

Sam finally came to join them at the table, but he sat on the chair as if folding in on himself.

Bob still glowered from his end of the table.

"So, what are you doing now, Kevin?" Charlotte dropped

the question into the thick, heavy quiet as she poured him a cup of coffee.

Kevin shot her a glance of gratitude. "I'm working construction now. Worked oil rigs for a few months. That's where the money is, but I've been thinking of settling down."

"You're lucky," Charlotte said, working her way around the table to sit next to Bob. "Not many construction companies have been hiring lately over here."

"Friend of a friend." Kevin laughed, but it was an empty sound, devoid of true humor. "Helps to have connections."

"Who are you anyway?" Jennifer sat down, dropped her elbows on the table, and cupped her chin, staring at him with interest.

"My name is Kevin Slater," Kevin said. "I'm Sam, Emily, and Christopher's father."

Jennifer rocked her head from side to side, as if looking at him from all angles. "You don't look like a deadbeat."

From the mouths of babes, Charlotte thought as she struggled to voice a coherent reprimand. "Jennifer . . . take . . . take your elbows off the table, honey." Charlotte sputtered. "And honey, we don't talk like that."

"My daddy does," Jennifer said, nonchalantly doing what Charlotte had told her to do. "So does my mommy." Jennifer pursed her lips. "What *is* a deadbeat anyway?"

Though Charlotte had thought much the same as Bill, and though Charlotte had her own feelings about Kevin Slater, he was currently a guest in their house, and he was sitting with his children. Who knew how many other gems her granddaughter had gleaned from overheard conversations from her parents?

"Pete, why don't you take Madison and Jennifer out for

a ride to Hannah's place? She was hoping to see the girls." A patent untruth, but she knew her dear friend would gladly have the girls over unannounced and would happily spoil them with whatever she had in the house. Pete could fill in the blanks for Hannah as to why the sudden and unexpected visit.

Pete shot her an annoyed glance, but she drilled her gaze into his, and he retreated. "Sure. C'mon girls. Let's go visit Aunt Hannah." He slurped down his still-hot coffee, grabbed a cookie, and slouched toward the porch.

"When are we visiting our mom?" Madison asked, obediently getting off her chair.

"We'll go after church tomorrow," Charlotte said. "I'm sure she'll be glad to see you." A moment of silence followed as the girls followed Pete to the porch.

"Who are those kids?" Kevin asked.

"Bill's," Charlotte said. "I'm taking care of the girls because his wife, Anna, just had a baby..." Her words drifted off in a wave of guilt. She was going to phone Bill again to find out what was happening with Anna and little Will. But in the excitement of the snowmobile and Kevin's visit, Anna and her newest grandson had completely slipped out of her mind.

"I see." More silence.

Charlotte's glance ticked over Emily and Sam. She knew that hundreds of questions were burning to be spoken by them. She knew because she had heard many of them—some shouted in anger, some whispered in pain.

But now the older children were tongue-tied in the actual presence of the man about whom they had wondered time and time again. The man who they had initially thought would come riding in to save them from moving from their home in San Diego to the backwoods of Bedford.

Christopher, the one who had been trying to make conversation, was now concentrating fiercely on his hot chocolate, stirring it with slow, deliberate movements.

Emily looked down at her hands, and Sam crumbled a cookie into his cup, avoiding his father's gaze.

"More coffee, Kevin?" she asked.

"Sure. Thanks." He looked around the kitchen. "I'm trying to remember the last time I was here at the farm."

"I'm sure you can't recall," Sam blurted out. "Must have been years ago."

Charlotte bit her lip from reprimanding Sam. Now that the girls were gone, she knew that some things had to come out. Kevin couldn't simply waltz back into their lives without any warning and not expect some repercussions. But she also knew she'd have to do some refereeing on the fly.

"I think Denise and I were dating," Kevin said.

"You can remember that?" Sam asked.

"Yeah. Sure. I remember a lot."

"Like what?" Sam asked. "Like where we lived in San Diego? How come you never came back to visit us? Never came back to see us?" Sam's tone grew surly, but a quick glance from Charlotte made him temper his attitude.

"I know I wasn't the best dad, but I've changed. Grown up."

"About time." Sam dropped back in his chair and crossed his arms over his chest.

"Hey, I've had my own stuff to deal with," Kevin replied, a note of exasperation entering his voice.

"I'm sure." Sam tilted his chair back on two legs, rocking angrily. "I'm sure you've had so many problems that your own kids were just an inconvenience."

"That's not true," Kevin shot back. "I wanted to come..." His sentence drifted off into the silence.

Charlotte felt surprised at Sam's anger. He had been the strongest proponent for finding their father. He had been the one who had spent the most time seeking him out.

And now that his father had actually shown up, he seemed to be the one with the most anger.

Kevin squirmed a bit and then he looked up. "Like I said, I've changed. I know I haven't been the best father, but I want to be your father now. I want to make up for all the things I did wrong. I want things to be different from now on."

Charlotte sat immobile, her every nerve ending quivering with fear. Did he mean to try and take the children from them? Was that how he wanted things to be different?

Silence greeted that remark.

Then Bob leaned forward.

"When did you find out about Denise?"

His soft-spoken question carried the weight of the grief they had all endured over the past twenty months. The months since Denise died.

"I heard...I heard through the grapevine. When they were organizing my class reunion." Kevin fiddled with his cup, turning it around and around. "And I'm sorry...sorry I didn't call sooner. But like I said, I had my own stuff to deal with."

At least he had the grace to look ashamed, Charlotte thought. For a moment, she wondered if he had, in his own way, struggled to find a way to handle the loss. If he had grieved in his own way.

"She died in a car accident," Sam said. "And you didn't know?"

Kevin shook his head. "I only heard about it, like I said, a half a year ago. And then, of course, you kids were gone already. I figured you didn't need me coming into your life right then."

More silence followed.

Charlotte glanced from Emily to Christopher, wondering what they were thinking. And again, she sent up quick prayers.

"So, Kevin, what are your plans? How long are you staying?" Charlotte knew the question needed to be voiced and the sooner the better.

Kevin ran his thumb up and down the side of his mug. "I've got about two or three weeks. I'm staying in a hotel close by because I wanted to spend some time with my kids."

Charlotte swallowed against a sudden pain. *My kids*. How quickly he swooped in to take ownership. She'd woven such daydreams around this Christmas season. She should have known better. Man plans, and God laughs.

"So what do we do now?" Sam asked, rocking in his chair. "Act as if nothing happened? As if everything is normal?"

Kevin shook his head. "No. But we can start somewhere. I'd like to take you kids out. Tomorrow—"

"We have church tomorrow," Christopher blurted out, daring to speak again. "We always go to church. Do you?"

Kevin shifted in his chair and shook his head. "No. I don't go anymore."

Christopher nodded, as if adding that bit of information to his mental file cabinet.

"But I could go tomorrow. We could get together after church."

Bob drew in a long sigh and leaned forward. "I think we need to talk a bit more about plans. But not right now."

Kevin frowned but seemed to catch the underlying message in Bob's words. Bob wasn't letting Kevin off that easy; Charlotte knew the three of them would have to sit down, without the children, and talk a few things out.

"Where are you staying?" Bob asked.

Kevin told him.

"Charlotte and I will come and see you later tonight. And we can talk a bit more." Then Bob got up and ambled to the family room, dropped into his recliner, and turned on the television.

Kevin emitted a short laugh. "Are you trying to get rid of me?"

"Stay as long as you want," Bob said. "I'm going to watch the news."

The television clicked on. Sam pushed himself back from the table, and left. Emily followed.

"Christopher, why don't you go and clean your room. I noticed that you didn't finish that job yesterday."

Christopher looked like he was about to object, but a knowing glance from Charlotte sealed the deal. He sighed and then trudged up the stairs. Charlotte could hear him hesitating on the landing, as if hoping to listen in.

"Make sure you sort out your laundry too," Charlotte added, just so he knew she understood what he was doing.

Charlotte waited until she heard the door to his bedroom click shut before she turned back to Kevin.

"What's with these kids?" Kevin asked. "I thought they'd be happy to see me."

I thought so too, Charlotte thought, surprised at their behavior.

"This is quite a shock for them, Kevin, your just showing up without any notice."

"I tried to call."

The hang-ups. Her phone stalker.

"You could have said something. Anything that would have given us some kind of warning. Some indication of what you wanted to do," she said.

Kevin looked down at his empty cup, sliding it back and forth between his hands, ignoring her comment. "So now what?"

"I think you should probably go back to your hotel, and tonight, as he said, Bob and I will come and visit you. We'll talk in private. Without the children around."

Kevin nodded slowly.

"Okay. Then I'll see you tonight." He scraped his chair back with an abrupt motion and then walked out the door without another word.

A few moments later Charlotte heard his truck start up.

And then she started to tremble.

Chapter Six

Christopher leaned his forehead against the glass, watching the bright red truck leave the driveway, a plume of white exhaust billowing up behind it.

He got down and sat on the floor, leaning against the wall. He pulled Lightning onto his lap, and the cat kneaded Christopher's pants with her feet, turned around and then settled down, her soft purrs vibrating against Christopher's stomach.

Their dad was back. And he thought Christopher was strong. That made him smile a bit.

Emily sat on the other end of Christopher's bed, her arms crossed over her chest, looking at Sam, who slouched on the floor facing Christopher, his wrists resting on his bent knees, his fingers tapping his shin. Sam spoke first. "I can't believe he just showed up without letting us know. Without saying anything. How does he think that works?"

"I just don't get why *you're* so mad, Sam." Emily sat up and pushed her long hair behind her ears. "You're the one who went running all over the country trying to find him."

"Well, maybe that's why I'm mad. Because maybe I learned that he wasn't going to come looking for us. And now he did —when it's convenient for him."

"Hey, Christopher, how are you doing?" Emily asked.

Christopher hugged his legs just a bit harder. Sam and Emily kept asking him how he felt about their dad coming back, and he couldn't say anything. A bunch of months ago, he thought his dad had left their family because of him. Because he cried so much. But his friend Dylan told him that all babies cry, so that meant his dad must have left because of something else.

He also had thought that when their dad came, he would only want Emily and Sam. But he'd told Christopher he was strong. That he could probably use Christopher's help. That had made Christopher feel special. But he didn't want to tell Emily and Sam that, because they seemed to be mad at their dad.

"Is he gone yet?" Emily asked.

Christopher nodded, stroking Lightning.

Sam sighed and pushed his hands through his hair like he did when he was frustrated. "Why did he have to come now? There are too many things going on. Why couldn't he come when it worked better for me?"

"Like when?" Emily sounded snappy again.

"Like when I'm ready to graduate? Move out?"

"So you would stay with Dad if he asked you to?"

Sam shrugged like he wasn't sure, and Christopher felt a slow pain starting to build in his stomach. Would Sam leave him? And if Sam left, would Emily follow him? Would they both leave him here alone on the farm?

But he didn't want to leave the farm.

He pulled Lightning up and held her tight. He had her and Toby to take care of, calves to feed, and all kinds of other things to do on the farm. And he'd promised Uncle

Pete he would help him plan his new house. He couldn't leave now even if his dad did need his help.

Now his stomach really hurt. He closed his eyes and started praying in his head like Grandma had taught him to.

Dear Jesus, I know you hear me because Grandma says You do even if I don't talk out loud or just whisper. I don't want to leave Grandma and Grandpa and Uncle Pete and Toby and the cats. I want to stay here and take care of the animals. But now my dad is here, and he's really nice. And I don't know what to do.

He felt like he was going to cry. He swallowed down some tears. He was going to be strong. Like his dad said he could be. And he was going to believe that Jesus would hear his prayer.

Emily and Sam talked for a while longer about their dad and then left. Christopher stayed in his room. He didn't want to go downstairs, and he didn't want to play outside.

Then he thought of the idea he had talked about with Uncle Pete this morning, when they were working on the snowmobile. About helping Uncle Pete design his house.

He pushed himself up and dug through his desk. He found some papers, some pencils, and his ruler. And then he started working because it was easier to plan Uncle Pete's house than to think about what would happen now that their dad was back.

He worked hard at his project, drawing houses, making plans, until he heard a truck coming up the driveway again. It was Uncle Pete coming back with Jennifer and Madison.

"Who's coming with me to cut down the Christmas tree?" he heard Uncle Pete yell into the house.

Christopher ran down the stairs. "I'm going to help you."

"Sam, Emily? Are you guys coming too?" Pete yelled even louder.

Grandma shushed him, putting a finger to her lips, and then pointed into the family room. Grandpa was fast asleep on the recliner.

Christopher was putting on his coat when Sam and Emily came down the stairs.

"Grandma, are you coming too?" Christopher asked as he sat on the bench and tugged his boots on.

"Of course she's coming," Uncle Pete said, grabbing Grandma's barn coat off the coat hook. "We're doing this together." He kicked off his boots, walked into the house, and stopped by Grandpa's recliner. He gave Grandpa a small shake. "Dad, wake up. We're getting the Christmas tree."

Christopher could hear Grandpa grumbling, but it sounded like he was coming along too.

"Sam, Emily, let's get those clothes on." Uncle Pete pulled on his gloves and yanked his hat over his ears. "C'mon. Let's get going. Mom, everybody, we have an important mission to accomplish."

Uncle Pete seemed to be the most excited about getting a Christmas tree, Christopher thought.

"And tomorrow we're visiting my new little brother," Jennifer said as Christopher helped her put on her mittens. "I got a present for him from Auntie Hannah. He's going to really like it. It's a pretty sweater that she made herself."

"And Grandma's making a really nice quilt for him," Madison added.

"Is everybody ready? I'm getting the ax." Uncle Pete left, and everyone followed him. "Come on, people; let's get a move on."

And then they were walking, all together, Grandpa telling them where they had to go to get the tree. Uncle Pete followed them with the snowmobile, still pulling the inner tube. He said they could tie the tree to the tube to bring it home.

Toby joined them, tail wagging.

"Toby looks like she's smiling," Jennifer said.

"And she should. She's got a great life," Uncle Pete said. "I think I'd like to be a dog too sometimes."

"I'd like to be a cat. They sleep a lot," Sam said with a laugh.

And soon they were talking about pets and cats and animals and remembering funny stories about Toby, and Christopher thought it seemed like the visit from his father hadn't even happened.

He wondered what his dad was doing this afternoon. Wondered if he was getting a Christmas tree. Wondered if he was going to get any presents.

And he felt a bit sorry for his dad.

"BEST TREE EVER," Emily said, standing back from the Christmas tree. Red, blue, yellow, and green lights twinkled in the branches, and brightly colored ornaments hung all over it, from top to bottom.

Christopher looked up from the popcorn he was stringing. Madison and Jennifer were supposed to help, but they had gotten tired of it so he was on his own. He didn't mind. It was his idea, after all.

The tree did look good, and once they got the popcorn string on, it would look even better.

"Just needs one last thing," Uncle Pete said, pulling the Christmas angel out of an old, dented box. He climbed up on a chair to put the angel on top of the tree. "Is she straight?" he asked.

"A little to the left," Sam said, looking up from his book. Pete moved it.

"Actually, a bit more to the right," Sam said.

Christopher caught Sam winking at him as Uncle Pete followed Sam's instructions. His brother was teasing Uncle Pete, but Christopher didn't say anything. Uncle Pete could tease them all pretty good, so it didn't hurt if he got teased back.

"One last thing to do before Grandpa and I have to leave," Grandma said, setting one last box in the living room. "The Christmas stockings."

"Can I hang them up?" Christopher asked, pushing the half-empty bowl of popcorn away. He could finish that later.

"Of course you can." Grandma gave him a big smile.

He pulled the first patchwork stocking out of the box. His name was embroidered on the cuff. "I think these are really neat," he said, holding it up, looking for the red-gingham square Grandma had told him was cut from a dress his mom wore on her first birthday.

"Can you tell us some more stories about the stockings?" Christopher brought his over to Grandma, whose smile got kind of soft and mushy when she took it from him. She must be remembering his mother, he thought, wishing he had more memories of her.

All he could remember was the smell of her perfume, how she would dance around the room with him when her favorite song played on the radio, and the way she would rub the top of his head whenever she tucked him in at night.

"I remember this dress," Grandma said, touching a yellow patch with tiny green leaves. "I bought the material at your Aunt Rosemary's shop, Fabrics and Fun. I couldn't afford much so I got her to cut a little less than the pattern called for. It was supposed to have long sleeves, but I ran out of material, so it ended up being a short-sleeved dress. Your mother looked so cute in it."

Christopher pointed to an orange patch. "What about this one?"

"That was a shirt that I bought for your mom when she was about seven. She saw it in a store and insisted on having it. Grandpa finally bought it for her. She wore it all the time until she ripped the sleeve out."

"Did she ever tell you how she ripped it?" Pete asked, stepping off the chair.

Grandma shook her head, and Christopher guessed a funny story about his mom was coming.

"I saw her riding one of the horses. The old one that Dad kept around for ages and ages. Think his name was Roany. But little as she was, she got a halter on that horse, brought it over to the fence, and then climbed on."

"She would have been the size of Madison. How did she get a halter on a horse?" Emily asked.

"Roany was so quiet, he would put his head down whenever Denise wanted to put the halter on."

"How did she get on Roany?" Sam asked.

"She'd just lead him to a fence, then climb up on the fence, and get on the horse from there."

"So how did she rip her shirt?" Christopher asked, trying to imagine Madison riding a horse by herself, much less putting a halter on it.

"Roany wouldn't go as fast as she wanted." Uncle Pete grabbed a handful of popcorn from the bowl and sat down on the couch. "So Denise was kicking and kicking Roany in the side with her little rubber boots, trying to get him to go over to the bushes so she could pull a branch off to hit him with. She finally got him to the willow bushes. She got hold of that branch in one hand and all of a sudden, Roany started walking away. But Denise wouldn't let go of the branch and wouldn't let go of the halter rope. Roany kept going, and Denise was slowly slipping sideways off the horse. Finally she fell and ripped her shirt. She was so mad at Roany. I can still see her stamping her feet in her rubber boots, yelling at him."

"What did Roany do?" Christopher asked.

"He just stopped, looked over at her, and then walked back to the corral where the other horses were." Pete laughed. "Denise finally pulled a branch off and chased Roany, trying to hit him with it. But it was so little, it didn't make any difference. She could be so stubborn." Pete popped some popcorn in his mouth, shaking his head.

"Sounds like someone else I know," Sam said, looking over at Emily.

"You should know," Emily said, making a face at him. She got up. "I think we need some gingerbread men. We didn't have dessert after supper. Can I put some out, Grandma?"

Grandma nodded and looked at her watch. Christopher knew that meant she was getting ready to go.

She and Grandpa were going to see their dad.

"And hot chocolate?" Jennifer asked, jumping up from the game she and Madison were playing, knocking over the bowl of popcorn. Christopher sighed. It was going to take him a long time to clean that all up.

"But we're not finished," Madison complained.

Christopher looked down at his stocking, imagining his mother as a little girl, sitting on top of a horse, kicking him with her rubber boots. In the story his mom was smaller than he was now.

He wished he knew how to ride a horse, he thought as he hung up the stocking. Then he gathered up the popcorn so he could start stringing it again.

Grandma and Grandpa came back to the living room. They were wearing their coats, and Grandma was pulling on her gloves. "We're leaving now. Madison and Jennifer, make sure you have a bath tonight. Emily, can you help them with their hair after their bath? Just braid it and roll up the ends in a couple of sponge rollers." Grandma gave a few more directions, even though everyone knew exactly what they had to do.

Grandpa just stood behind her, rocking back and forth, like he was nervous.

Christopher felt the ache coming back into his stomach. He knew they were on their way to see his dad, wherever he was staying. He wondered what they were going to talk about.

They said good-bye and left. Christopher headed upstairs to call it a night. Maybe things would make more sense in the morning.

Chapter Seven

"And how are we going to do this?" Charlotte clutched the handles of her purse on her lap as she stared at the door of the motel room where their son-in-law was staying.

She and Bob still sat in her car, dwarfed by Kevin's bright red truck. Exhaust from their car swirled around them, lit up by the light from Kevin's motel room.

Ever since she and Bob had taken the children in, she'd imagined many confrontations with Kevin, but she'd never imagined one would take place in the Bedford Motel.

The whole scene felt cheap. Tawdry. Like something out of a detective movie.

"We find out what he wants, and we figure out what we have to do from there." Bob seemed remarkably calm, considering that the man waiting in the room in front of them held so much in his hands.

"And what if he wants the children?" As she voiced the dreaded thought, her heart thumped heavily in her chest.

"Then we deal with that." Bob's shoulders lifted in a huge sigh as he turned off the car's engine. "We'll just have to pray it won't come to that."

"I've been doing enough of that lately," Charlotte said, slipping her gloves on and opening the car door.

From inside the room, Charlotte heard the forced enthusiasm of a television commercial promising peace of mind if one used that brand of household cleanser.

If only it were that easy, Charlotte thought. *If only we could wash all our troubles away with a pail of water and a capful of Wonder Clean.*

Bob knocked on the door. The sound of the television was muted before the door opened.

For the space of a couple of heartbeats they all stood in the doorway, facing each other, sizing each other up. Kevin had changed into a blue dress shirt and gray dress pants. His hair was still damp and his freshly shaved face shone.

He looked like he was trying to create a favorable impression.

"Come in," he said, standing aside.

The room was small but had two chairs and a small table. Kevin had set out two cups on the table and a couple of napkins.

"I made a pot of coffee, if you're interested," he said, closing the door behind them.

Charlotte glanced quickly around the room, trying not to look like she was prying. She could see Kevin's suitcase pushed against one wall. The door to the bathroom was open and the mirror was still foggy from his shower.

She knew he'd moved around a lot. She also knew he'd been living with another woman for a time.

Now he was here. Staying in a motel.

And for the tiniest moment she felt sorry for him.

"Please, sit down," Kevin said gesturing to the table. He waited until Charlotte gingerly seated herself on the edge of the chair and then pulled the small pot of coffee from the coffeemaker.

She allowed him to pour her a cup and Bob did the same. Kevin put the coffeepot back and then dropped onto the bed across from them as she and Bob ripped open packets of sweetener and stirred them into their coffee.

A heavy silence reigned, and then Bob cleared his throat. A simple thing. An ordinary precursor to many talks. But here, now, it had an ominous sound, heralding the foray into unfamiliar and frightening territory.

"So. We need to find out what your intentions are," Bob said, holding his coffee cup between both hands, frowning at his son-in-law.

Kevin crossed his arms over his chest, his foot tucked under his knee. "I just want to see my kids."

"For how long? And how often?" Charlotte asked, keeping her voice quiet to offset the roaring in her ears.

"Like I said, I'm off for the next three weeks. I thought I could have them for Christmas. I haven't had a Christmas with my kids since . . ." He frowned, as if trying to remember.

"Since you left Denise when Christopher was a baby," Bob put in.

"I guess." A limp shrug followed his equally limp reply.

"We have our own plans for the holiday season, you do realize," Bob said, taking over the conversation in a way that surprised Charlotte.

"And I want to take them shopping." Kevin shot them a quick smile, ignoring Bob's comment. "Got money burning a hole in my pocket, and I want to make up for lost time. Thought maybe I could take them tomorrow. I know you go to church, but I could pick them up afterward. Take them out."

So easily he insinuated himself into their lives. As if he had never been gone. As if the gap of nine years didn't yawn between them.

"Why now, Kevin? Why, after all these years, are you coming back now into these children's lives? They haven't heard a thing from you for over nine years. You didn't send Denise any kind of financial support the entire time you were gone, and you didn't even give her one ounce of moral support. She was literally on her own—"

"I know all that." Kevin held his hand up to stop her. "And I feel rotten about that. I haven't been a great father, but I want to make that better. I want to be a good father for my children now. And I know I can."

Charlotte pressed her anger back and folded her hands tightly in her lap. Kevin's excuses came so quickly, so easily—it was as if he had rehearsed them in front of the mirror before they got there.

Please, Lord, help me not to lose my temper with him and his shallow replies.

"How do you propose to do that?" Bob asked.

"Like I said, I want to be involved. I want to spend time with them. I can give you money if you want . . ."

"We don't need any of your money." Bob spoke quietly but with a heavy authority that Kevin seemed to understand.

"Of course," he said, pulling in on himself.

"And you still haven't answered Charlotte's question."

Kevin gave them a puzzled frown.

Bob folded his hands, resting his elbows on his knees, and leaned forward, confronting Kevin man to man.

"Why now?"

The two simple words, heavy in their import, seemed to echo off the walls.

Kevin looked away, a flicker of shame in his eyes.

"I told you—"

"You told us what you think we want to hear. But what I want to hear is the truth," Bob said, a determined edge to his voice.

Charlotte felt a surge of pride at Bob's self-possession. Though he and Pete knocked heads over the farm and what to do, Bob wasn't, on the whole, a confrontational person. He preferred to come at things sideways, rather than head-on. But now it seemed, when it came to the welfare of the grandchildren, Bob was going to fight.

Kevin sighed and pinched the bridge of his nose. "Okay. Truth is, I heard about Denise's death just a little while ago. Like I told you. And I figured that, well, if she was gone, maybe I had a chance with the kids."

"What do you mean?" Charlotte asked.

Kevin shrugged. "Denise and I didn't always agree on how to raise the kids. And she wasn't the easiest person to live with."

"Be very careful," Bob warned.

Kevin looked taken aback and held his hands up in a gesture of surrender. "Okay, I probably shouldn't have said that, but, you know, it's hard when you're kind of just getting by with two kids and kind of living hand to mouth... Then there's a third kid that wasn't planned, and I just couldn't deal with all of it."

Charlotte felt as if she had been doused with ice water.

Ever since he could put things together, Christopher had secretly thought his father had left because of him.

And now Kevin was virtually saying that was true.

Christopher absolutely could not find this out.

"And now you can deal with it?" Bob was asking.

Kevin got up from the bed, walked over to the counter and took a swig of pop from a bottle sitting there. "I think I can."

"Think?"

"Okay. I'm sure I can. And when I heard about Denise's death, I knew I had to be there. For the kids."

He turned to them, his expression almost pleading. "I want a chance with them. I want to connect with them. I haven't got anyone else."

For another tiny moment, Charlotte felt sorry for him. "They aren't like a pet that you can use to assuage your loneliness," she warned. "They come with their own baggage and needs."

Kevin pointed his bottle toward her. "I've lived with them. I know what I need to do."

Charlotte doubted that, but for now she had to set that aside. She didn't want to fight with Kevin. Not now. Not when so much hung in the balance.

"Okay. So how do you see this playing out?" Bob was asking. "We need to lay out some ground rules."

Kevin paced the small section of floor between the counter and the bed. "Okay. I figure I take the kids out tomorrow. Spend some time with them. Take them out shopping in Harding. Looks like there's some decent stores there. Then I'd like to have them over a weekend—I could pick them up next Saturday evening and bring them back Sunday night. That's next week." He took another swig from the bottle. "How does that work for you two?"

"We'll need to discuss this with the children," Bob said.

Kevin frowned. "Why? This is what I need to do. I've got lots of time to make up with them, and I want to get started as soon as possible. I'd think they would want to spend time with their long-lost dad."

Kevin seemed confident of the children's positive reaction to his sudden reappearance in their lives. Charlotte wasn't sure that was the case, but she wasn't getting into a discussion about that here and now.

"How can we get hold of you?" Bob asked, pulling a pen and paper out of his pocket.

Kevin rattled off a number and repeated it when Bob didn't get it the first time.

Bob put the paper back into his coat pocket and then got up.

"You're leaving already?" Kevin asked.

"We don't have much else to discuss," Bob said.

"What do you mean?" Kevin released a bitter laugh that sent a shiver of premonition down Charlotte's spine. "I'm around for more than this week, you know. You said nothing about next week. Or Christmas."

"I think we'll play this week by week," Bob said quietly. "When we see how this week goes with the children, then we'll discuss Christmas."

"That's fine and dandy. We can put that off, but you may as well know, I'm not here just to visit with my kids. I have other plans. Bigger plans."

As Kevin's gaze flicked from Bob to Charlotte and then back again, the premonition became a sliver of dread.

"What kind of plans?" Charlotte hesitated to ask.

Kevin stood up and glanced from Charlotte to Bob, his eyes narrowed, as if he meant business.

"I've talked to a lawyer. I have plans to get my kids back. For good."

Chapter Eight

For the first five minutes of the drive back home, neither Bob nor Charlotte broke the ominous silence in the car. It was as if both of them were in shock and trying to process their own thoughts before either could speak them aloud.

Charlotte's mind was a morass of fear, loaded with half-formulated questions and dread.

How could Kevin think ... What was he thinking? ... Surely he didn't ... But he seemed so confident.

Again and again his words replayed in her mind, growing with intensity each time around.

For good. Getting the kids back. For good.

Bob reached across the car and closed his large hand over her icy one. He squeezed it and sighed.

"He doesn't have much of a chance, you know," he said.

Charlotte wasn't sure. "I should have worked more on protecting our guardianship when I went to visit that lawyer in Harding last May. I should have followed through on that." Panic threaded her voice as she spoke. "If I had solidified our claim, he wouldn't stand a chance."

She pressed her lips together to keep the sorrow that filled her heart from spilling out. It wouldn't do any good if she cried in front of Bob. She needed to be strong. Needed to trust that God wouldn't put these children into their lives only to take them away.

"He doesn't even have a place to live," Bob said. "Apparently he has a steady job now, but who knows? He hasn't been a part of their lives since Christopher was a baby. He hasn't sent money. We've been a steady, stable home for them for nearly two years."

Charlotte turned her hand and clutched Bob's as she drew in a shuddering breath. "I'm scared, Bob. He's their father. We're just their grandparents. And we didn't spend much time with the kids before they came here either."

Bob was silent for a moment. "I can't think about losing those kids..." He stopped there, and Charlotte thought she would cry at the pain in his voice. If he broke, she would as well. And then where would they be? Two old people, sobbing in a tiny little car.

"I have to talk to that lawyer, Marcus Lindstrom, as soon as possible. I need to see about getting our rights in order." Charlotte looked ahead into the swirling snow, the flakes growing shiny and large, magnified by the tears gathering in her eyes. She blinked and felt moisture slide down her cheeks.

Please, Lord ... was all she could pray. At one time—it now seemed eons ago—she'd prayed for Kevin Slater. Prayed that God would watch over him and protect him.

Now she didn't know what to pray.

"I thought you held off on that suit because you weren't

sure if you wanted to make that decision for the children." Bob's voice held the sting of reprimand, and it was all Charlotte could do not to respond to his tone rather than this words.

"I did it because I didn't want the children to find out that he wouldn't even fight for his paternal rights at that time. I didn't want them to consider that as one more rejection from him." Her reasons had seemed so sound at the time. So sensitive and well thought out.

Now they seemed foolish and overly sentimental.

"Marcus said we had a strong case then," Charlotte continued, struggling to keep her voice even. "I think we have an even stronger case now. We have to fight this. I can't stand to think that he might get them, Bob," she cried, her emotions spiraling out of control. "They're our children now more than his."

A moment of silence followed her outburst, broken only by the static of the radio that had fallen off-channel and the swish of the windshield wipers across the glass.

"I think we always need to remind ourselves that they are first and foremost God's children." Bob spoke quietly, but it seemed to Charlotte that he had to convince himself of the sentiment as much as he had to convince her.

She felt humbled by his comment.

"You're right. I keep forgetting that even our own children were really just ours to raise for the Lord. That He claimed them first." Charlotte sighed, folding her hands tightly together, as if to contain her runaway thoughts. "I have to constantly remind myself to put their needs first."

"And if they need their father . . ." Bob's words trailed off.

Charlotte sighed, pressing her lips together. She didn't want to finish the thought.

Please, Lord, she prayed again. *Give us strength to deal with whatever comes our way. Help us to remember, as Bob said, that these children are Yours first.*

"So what do we tell the children?" she asked as they approached the turnoff to the farm.

Bob clicked on the turn signal and slowed down. "The same thing we told Kevin. We're taking this one week at a time."

Charlotte wasn't sure the children would appreciate that, but at the same time she knew Bob was right. No sense in giving them false hope or false plans. Regardless of what Kevin said now, his past actions hadn't shown him to be very responsible.

Time would tell whether or not he could follow through on his plans.

Chapter Nine

During Advent, we wait. Wait for the coming of a promise. Wait for the fulfilling of a yearning. We know that this world is not everything and that there is a promise of other things to come." Pastor Evans glanced around the congregation, his hands clutching the pulpit, his expression earnest.

Emily knew she should be paying closer attention, but she couldn't help glancing to the side where her friend Ashley sat.

With Ryan and Ryan's sister.

Emily wanted things back to the way they had been. She and Ashley hanging out, sharing gossip and sharing clothes. Not sharing time with her boyfriend. She had so much she wanted to tell Ashley, but she hadn't had a chance.

Last night she'd tried to call her, but her mom had said she was out with Ryan.

So she had hoped she could talk to her this morning. At church. All the stuff with her dad was still rolling around in her head, and she wanted—no, needed to talk to her friend.

Emily shot another look at Ashley, trying to figure out what was going on. On Friday, at school, Ashley had worn a tight T-shirt and low-cut pants, the kind of clothes Emily used to wear more often when she first came here. The kind Ashley told her made her look cheap.

And today she wore a pile of makeup and giggled with Ryan's sister Malinda as if they were best friends.

Things were just getting too weird in her life, Emily thought, slumping farther down in her pew.

"You're supposed to sit still," Madison said from beside her.

Emily tugged playfully on her cousin's hair. Madison could be a pain, but Emily had learned not to take her too seriously.

She tried to turn her attention back to Pastor Evans, but she'd lost where he was going. The last thing he'd said was something about yearning and waiting.

Well, there was one thing she didn't need to wait for anymore and that was for their dad to come back. He was here now.

Last night, after Grandma and Grandpa came back from visiting him, they didn't say much except that he was taking them out after they visited Anna in the hospital.

She wasn't so sure she wanted to go.

Yesterday, after she, Sam, and Christopher had had their little talk, she'd been turning things over and over in her head. Why had their dad come back now? What did he want?

She thought of the farm, thought of her friends. Did she really want to go with him? She barely knew him.

Not that long ago, Sam had run away to find their dad, and now it seemed he didn't know what he wanted. And

Emily was even less sure. Should she go along with Sam? Should she make up her own mind? What if Sam wanted to go and she didn't? What if Christopher didn't want to go and she did?

Emily sighed and smoothed her hands over her new skirt. She'd had such fun making it and had looked forward to showing it to Ashley.

It all seemed so unimportant now.

Beside her, Madison was standing up, and with a start Emily realized the service was almost over. They sang a song, listened to the minister give them a blessing, telling them to go in peace and to take the peace of Christ out into the world this week.

She waited as long as she thought was polite and then scooted past Sam to catch up to Ashley. She really wanted to talk to her friend.

"Hey, Ash. How are you?" Emily asked, tucking her one arm into Ashley's, trying to act as if everything was normal. "Hey, Malinda." She leaned forward a bit, trying to catch Malinda's eye, but she was looking somewhere else.

Ashley squeezed her arm. "I'm good . . . sorry, Malinda, what did you want?"

Malinda whispered something in Ashley's ear. "Oh, you're just being silly," she said with a fake laugh.

"Sorry." Ashley turned back to Emily. "Hey, you finished your skirt. I really like it."

"Thanks. Did you get my message?"

"Message?" Ashley frowned, and then giggled as Malinda whispered something else in her ear. "I told you, forget it." She giggled again and turned back to Emily.

"What were you saying about a message?" Ashley asked, her cheeks flushed and her eyes bright. Then she giggled again and gave Malinda an elbow in the side. "Quit yakking at me. I'm trying to talk to my friend."

Ashley let go of Ryan's sister and focused on Emily. "Now, tell me about your message. Obviously my mom forgot to tell me. She's been kind of distracted lately."

"Don't take too long, Ash. We're supposed to be meeting up with Ryan and Ashton in a couple of minutes."

Ashley rolled her eyes at Emily's questioning glance. "Some kind of double date." Ashley shook Emily's arm. "So. Spill."

Emily gave Ashley a tight smile.

Right. Like she was going to spill everything here and now as people milled around them, talking and chatting, moving past them to get out.

"That's okay. I'll catch you later. Have fun this afternoon."

"What are you doing after church?"

"Going to visit Anna. She had her baby."

"Really?" Ashley squealed, sounding like her old friend again. "That's so cool!"

"A little boy."

"Ashley, are you coming?" Ryan called over the noise of the departing congregation.

"Just wait." Ashley turned back to Emily. "So, have you seen him yet?"

"No. I told you. We're going to visit him right now."

"Right. Sorry." Ashley gave her an apologetic smile and then squeezed her arm. "So what was the message?" she asked as she tossed a quick glance over her shoulder to where Ryan and his sister were waiting.

Emily wanted nothing more than to tell her friend about her dad. To spill out all her confusion and worry. To ask her what she was supposed to do.

Ever since she'd moved here, Ashley had become an even better friend than her friends in San Diego. She'd always felt she could tell Ashley everything or ask her anything.

But not anymore.

Right now Emily could tell that Ashley was getting fidgety. She was just being polite, asking questions and pretending to pay attention to her.

"I just wanted to...see...how you were doing," Emily said.

"I'm great. Just great." Ashley gave her a quick smile. "I'll give you a call later on. You home tonight?"

"I don't know." She had no idea how much time her father expected to spend with them or when they'd be home.

"Okay, then. Maybe at school tomorrow." Ashley fluttered her hands in a good-bye. "Later."

And then Ashley was gone, leaving Emily feeling all alone in a crowd of people.

"I THINK LITTLE WILL looks like me." Pete bent over the tightly wrapped bundle in Anna's arms and pushed his cap back on his head and grinned at Anna, as if checking to see what she would say.

Charlotte noted that Anna wasn't even looking at him. Her entire focus was on the baby she held close to her.

"I think he has Madison's nose," Anna murmured, touching the tip of his tiny nose with her finger.

"But he's got Jennifer's cheeks," Bill put in from beside his wife, his arm curled around Anna's shoulders, his entire attention on his son.

The serene look on his face made Charlotte's own heart ache just a little. Her mind so easily flashed back to Bob, holding each of their babies after they'd been born. He'd had the same expression on his face that Bill had now.

What dreams she and Bob had woven around each of them. Bill. Denise. Pete.

She looked back at Bill, now a father himself. Responsible. Important.

She let her mind linger on Denise a moment, but thinking of Denise led her to Kevin, and she didn't want him to spoil the moment.

And Pete, standing across from her, taller than Bob, was making plans to get married, and perhaps thinking of becoming a father himself one day.

"And now, the poor kid has his father's and his grandfather's names," Pete put in, shooting a teasing glance toward Bill.

But his brother was oblivious to his jibes, so taken was he with his young son.

"I want to see my cheeks on my brother again."

Bob lifted Jennifer up so she could see better. "He is adorable," Jennifer said with a theatrical sigh. "Can I hold him?"

Anna glanced from Jennifer to Charlotte, as if unsure of what to do.

"Why don't you wait until you and your mommy and your little brother are at home," Charlotte said. "Then you can sit on your couch and hold him properly."

Jennifer's mouth shifted into a pout as she rubbed her eyes and her bright red cheeks. "I want to hold him now." She looked tired—and no wonder. Pete had had them on the go all yesterday afternoon, trying to keep the children's minds off Kevin's visit. Cutting the tree down, dragging it home and decorating it. She figured that Pete had given in to the girls' demands to stay up just a bit longer while she and Bob were talking to Kevin.

And then church this morning and now here.

"If you hold your brother, then I don't get to hold you," Bob teased giving her a tight squeeze.

"You can hold me anytime you want, Grandpa," Jennifer said.

"Even when you're thirteen?"

"Yeah," she said, as if she couldn't imagine not being held in her grandfather's arms.

"You would be big," Bob returned.

"But I would still be your little girl, right?"

While Jennifer and Bob teased each other, Charlotte drew nearer to Anna, and with the tip of her forefinger, gently nudged the flannel sheet aside so she could see her newest grandson better.

His nose was a tiny button, his eyes just two folded wrinkles of eyelids, and his mouth formed a tiny little bow.

"How precious," she breathed, a gentle awe filling her at the sight of this very new grandchild.

"Do you want to hold him?" Anna shifted the soft bundle toward her.

Charlotte glanced at Jennifer, who was giggling at something Bob was telling her, and nodded. She didn't want to upset her granddaughter, but it looked as if she was busy for now.

Charlotte carefully drew the flannel bundle out of Anna's arms and gently adjusted him to hold him close to her. Then she bent over and drew in the gentlest breath, drawing in the delicate, slightly spicy scent of the new baby. Her heart stuttered for a moment as her memories sifted back to her own babies. Remembered so clearly their blue, unfocused eyes, the pursed lips with their tiny bubble of milk from nursing, the gentle warmth of them all bundled up in her arms.

"So precious," she murmured. "Grandma already loves you so much, little man." She gently laid her cheek against his as her mother's heart formed a prayer of protection for this fragile and amazing new life. "He is so beautiful," Charlotte said, nuzzling him again.

"Can I hold him, Grandma?" Emily asked, a soft smile curving her lips.

Babies, thought Charlotte, *bring out the mother in all young girls*.

"Of course you can," Charlotte said, moving around to where Emily stood.

"Are you sure she should?" Anna asked, fluttering her hands as if to take Will away from Charlotte.

Charlotte frowned slightly. "Emily is very careful."

Anna pressed her lips together, glanced at Emily, and then nodded.

"It's okay, Grandma. I don't need to," Emily said.

But Charlotte gently shifted the precious bundle over to her and smiled as Emily curved her arms around the baby, as if she had been doing it all her life.

Emily glanced at Anna, who was still frowning. Then Emily looked down at Will. A gentle smile curved her lips.

"He's so cute," Emily said, bending over to breathe in his newborn scent.

Charlotte stood beside her granddaughter and put her arm around her shoulders. "Pretty precious, isn't he?" she asked, giving her granddaughter a squeeze.

"His fingernails aren't any bigger than a grain of rice," Emily said with a note of awe in her voice. "And look, his eyelids are even smaller than my pinky nail."

She bent her head over him, holding him close.

Charlotte chanced a quick look at Anna and caught her daughter-in-law looking at Emily with an expression of such tenderness that it hooked on her heart.

Anna and Emily had not always gotten along so well in the past, so to see her usually uptight daughter-in-law smiling the way she was gave Charlotte hope for both of them.

"What's going on? There are too many people in here!"

An imperious voice from the doorway broke the silence, and Anna's mother strode into the room. Today she wore a long white coat, black leather boots that matched her purse, and leather gloves.

She tugged her gloves off, finger by finger, as her blue eyes flicked from Charlotte to Bob to Pete and then Sam and Christopher, who were already sidling toward the doorway, as if knowing what was about to descend on them.

Charlotte tried not to look at Emily but couldn't help catching her indiscreet eye-roll.

"My daughter just had a baby," Mrs. Adlai spoke with a calculated crispness, as if addressing a group of teenagers. "I assumed that the only visitors allowed were grandparents and siblings of the child?"

"The child being Will," Pete said in a laconic voice.

"Don't you think there are too many people in here, Charlotte?" Mrs. Adlai asked, her voice even but with an edge that made Charlotte feel uncomfortable.

"They can stay," Anna protested. "I already cleared it with the nurse."

"My dear, the nurse obviously can't see how worn out you look." Mrs. Adlai tugged the bedspread straight and smoothed out a couple of wrinkles. She moved aside the flowers Charlotte, Bob, and the children had brought and pulled a huge bouquet of rust-and-orange-colored roses to the front of the table.

"You should rest, my dear," Mrs. Adlai said, inserting herself between Charlotte and Anna. "And when you wake up we can freshen up your hair."

"I'm rested, and my hair is fine." But in spite of her protests, Anna lifted a hand to her head and tucked a wayward strand of hair behind her ear.

Charlotte was reluctant to leave, but she decided it would be better if she made things easier for Anna.

Mrs. Adlai glanced at Emily. "I'd like to hold my grandson, please," she said with a smile that didn't quite reach her voice. "My daughter and grandson need their rest." Mrs. Adlai tucked Will into her arms as her glance shifted from Emily to Charlotte and then the boys. She didn't say anything, but Charlotte could clearly read her expression. She wished everyone would leave.

"Well, we'd better be going," Bob mumbled. He said good-bye to Anna and shot a quick glance toward Pete, who got the hint.

"Let's make like a tree and leave," Pete said.

"But we just got here," Christopher complained. "And I didn't even have a chance to hold my new cousin."

"You will. Later. We gotta split, buddy. *Now*."

"I'll walk you to the door," Bill said, clearly glad for an excuse to get away from his mother-in-law for a while.

Mrs. Adlai said to Charlotte, "If you'll give me a moment, I'll walk down with you, and I can get the girls' suitcases."

"I don't want to go with Gran," Jennifer said, clinging to Emily's hand. "I want to stay on the farm."

"Young lady..." Mrs. Adlai began.

"Can we please stay until tonight?" Madison added, turning to her mother. "Please, Mommy?"

Anna glanced from her mother to her girls and then, to Charlotte's surprise, nodded.

"Sure, you can stay another day. If it's okay with Grandma Stevenson."

"It's fine with me," Charlotte said.

Mrs. Adlai frowned. "Anna, do you think it's a good idea to let them get their way like that?"

"The girls love it on the farm, and they don't get to spend nearly as much time with their cousins as they'd like. Besides, I could use your help here." Anna gave her mother a steady glance, as if to challenge her.

"I'll have to go to the farm to pick them up?" Mrs. Adlai asked, her voice prim.

"I don't mind bringing them back," Charlotte said, sensing this might be a problem. She looked at Mrs. Adlai. "Why don't you give me your cell phone number, and we can make arrangements?"

Mrs. Adlai blinked as if she didn't understand, but then she handed Will back to Anna, drew a gold pen out of her purse, scribbled her number inside a small leather book and ripped out the page.

Charlotte took the paper and gave her a smile. "Thank you. We'll see you tonight." And she put the paper in her pocket. "Jennifer, Madison, say good-bye to your mommy."

Emily held them up so they could kiss Anna and say good-bye to their little brother.

As soon as she put them down, though, they scurried out of the room without looking back, as if afraid their mother would change her mind about them going back to the farm.

"Bye, Aunt Anna." Emily gave Anna a quick wave. "We'll see you again."

Anna smiled at her and Charlotte took a chance, carefully squeezing past Mrs. Adlai to bend over Anna and kiss her forehead.

"Take care of yourself, my dear," she said quietly, gently brushing a strand of hair away from her face. "We'll come by the house once you're settled in."

Anna caught her hand and lowered her voice. "Bill said Kevin is back in town. Is that true?"

Charlotte nodded, not sure she wanted the entire family history spilled out in front of Anna's mother.

But Anna only nodded. "You can tell me more next time I see you."

Charlotte straightened, murmured a quick farewell to Anna's mother, and then left the room.

"I really wanted to stay awhile," Emily said, sounding wistful as they walked down the hallway. "I wanted to hold Will a little longer."

"I probably should have said something, Emily. I'm sorry," Charlotte said.

Emily glanced back at the room. "I guess I'll get a chance some other time." Then she sighed. "And now we get to see my dad. I wish . . ."

Charlotte struggled not to ask Emily what she wished. She wanted more than anything to give her granddaughter all kinds of advice about what to watch for, what to be wary of, but it wasn't her place.

"I think it's good that your father wants to be a part of your lives," she said, choosing to be encouraging and positive.

Emily shot her a puzzled look. "Really? I thought you didn't like him."

"He's your father," Charlotte said, struggling to formulate her thoughts in a diplomatic fashion. Yes, she'd had her troubles with Kevin. When Emily had found Denise's diary and had shared it with her, Charlotte had struggled once again with feelings of mistrust, of anger toward Kevin. But the reality was, this man wanted to be a part of his children's lives. "And I'm glad that he...is trying to be responsible."

Emily looked a bit puzzled but didn't say anything.

As they headed home, Charlotte couldn't help but wonder what Kevin would tell the children when he came to get them. Would he let them know he was going to fight for them? That he wanted them to stay with him?

Please, Lord, she prayed again. *Help him to keep his counsel for now. The children don't need any false promises or false hopes.*

And what if they weren't false?

Charlotte couldn't bear to think of that right now. One day at a time, she had told Bob, and she had to follow through on that.

Chapter Ten

"Pick whatever you want," their father said, handing out large menus. "Don't worry about the cost. I've got more than enough money to pay for dinner for all of you."

He said that like he was bragging.

Sam glanced around the restaurant. The waiters and waitresses wore black skirts or slacks and white shirts and ties. Soft music played in the background, and people were talking quietly.

The tablecloth he'd shoved his legs under was crisp and heavy and made a crinkle on his lap.

Ditto the napkin.

He glanced down at his faded blue jeans and wished he'd taken Grandma's advice and dressed up a bit.

Emily had ducked behind the massive menu, pretending she had some clue as to what was on it.

"How's school treating you kids?" their dad asked them as he put his own menu down on the table. "Probably kind of hokey compared to the school you went to in San Diego."

Emily didn't answer, and Christopher kept his head down, so Sam filled in the slack in the conversation. "It's okay. There are some good people there." He almost had to laugh at himself. He'd certainly never thought he'd see the day when he would be defending Bedford High School. Not that long ago he'd wanted to get as far away from Bedford as possible.

"Good. Good." Their dad nodded and gave them a funny smile, like he wasn't sure what else to say.

Sam turned back to the menu. All the way to the restaurant their dad had been the one talking, telling them all about the work he did and how he enjoyed traveling. Then he started in on how much he had missed them and how glad he was that he could visit them.

Sam shifted from being completely ticked off at his father to feeling confused, and he still wasn't sure where his feelings would land.

For years he and Emily had wondered where their dad was and what he was doing and why he had taken off on them. Now, all of a sudden, he shows up, and none of them knew what to do or what to think.

After the waiter took their order, an uncomfortable silence spread around the table. Sam felt like his brain had gone empty. Which was weird. He'd imagined sitting and talking with his dad so many times in the past few years. He'd had so many conversations with him in his head. But now that he was actually here, he couldn't think of anything to say, and his dad had already told them all about himself so there wasn't much to ask.

"What's up for next year?" their father asked them, leaning his elbows on the table and looking around from one kid to the other. "Sam, you'll be graduating, won't you?" he asked, now focusing on Sam. "Whatcha gonna do then?"

"I'm thinking of going to college."

"And thinking of going is all he's doing," Emily said, leaning back in her chair, fiddling with the black scarf she'd tied around her neck.

Sam shot her an angry look. Lately he felt that people were pushing him in all directions, and he didn't need any smart comments from his little sister. "I'm still not sure which college I want to go to."

"Why even bother with college? Why not work construction, like I do? You could make a lot of money. I could get you a job." Their dad grinned at Sam, but for some reason it made him feel uncomfortable.

"He has to go to college," Emily said, her purple nail polish flashing as she tapped her fingers against her arm. "His girlfriend is going, and he's got to be there with her."

"Girlfriend?" Their dad's mouth curved into a funny grin as he leaned a little closer to Sam. He nudged him with his elbow. "Tell me about this girl. Is she pretty?"

Thankfully Sam was spared from having to respond to the awkward question because just then the waiter arrived with their food. The next twenty minutes were taken up with eating. Their dad didn't ask him any more questions about Arielle, and no one else said anything either.

The food tasted really good, and their dad seemed to be okay with no one saying anything while they ate. When they were done, their dad snapped his fingers, and some guy wearing a black jacket over his shirt came pushing a cart full of desserts.

"Pick whatever you want," their dad said to them.

Christopher just shook his head, and Emily said no. Sam didn't want to be the only one eating dessert, so he said no too. Which was too bad. Some of the choices looked pretty awesome.

"Just give me the bill," their dad said, sounding a little peeved as he talked to the waiter.

He made a big show of pulling out his wallet and dropping a bunch of bills on the table. When the bill had been paid, they pulled on their coats and walked through a bitter wind to Kevin's truck.

Supper down, Sam thought. *What's next?*

"How can you guys stand this weather compared to San Diego?" their dad asked. "I can't believe you'd want to stay here in this cold. I'd die. I was so glad to get away from this place."

"It's not like we have a lot of choice," Sam said, though a small part of him felt a bit defensive about where he lived. Though he didn't always like the cold himself, there were things he did enjoy.

"How could it be good?" Their dad blew on his hands.

"Uncle Pete pulled us on a tube behind the snowmobile. That was fun," Christopher put in, obviously feeling a bit more comfortable than he had.

"Well, yeah. I guess." Their dad laughed, but it sounded to Sam more like he was poking fun at Christopher. While he walked he pressed a button on his keychain that started the truck and unlocked the doors. "Where's a good place to go shopping?" their dad asked.

"There's a mall at the end of Main Street," Sam offered as they climbed into the truck. He was getting tired of being the only one talking, but Emily had her stubborn face on and Christopher just looked nervous.

Luckily their dad turned the radio on when they got into

the truck, so no one had to say anything. By the time they got to the mall, Sam felt even more uncomfortable.

This guy was their dad. And no one knew what to say to him. And now he wanted to take them shopping. It was like every bad-father-and-kids movie he'd ever watched. Dad wants to make up for all the things he did, so let's go buy stuff.

"Guys, you'll have to let me know what you want." He threw his arms wide as they walked across the parking lot to the brightly lit mall. "It's open season, and it's open wallet. So let's go spend some money."

The mall was full of shiny colored Christmas decorations and people bustling around carrying shopping bags. Christmas music bounced out of speakers everywhere, and as Sam looked around, he felt as if he were back on familiar territory.

When he lived in San Diego, he and his friends always hung around the mall after school. Now, at Christmastime, this mall seemed like a familiar place, and he felt a familiar sense of expectation that the glittering lights and music created.

They walked past a bunch of stores; and then their dad stopped at an electronics store.

"Now I know there's got to be something here for you boys." Kevin looked from Sam to Christopher, and in his eyes Sam caught a bit of hesitancy. As if he weren't sure himself what to do.

"We'll start with you, Christopher," he said. "I have an idea what you might want."

Their dad walked over to the store's games section and found a salesman who didn't look a lot older than Sam himself. He wore a blue golf shirt with his name embroidered on the pocket.

"What's the latest gadget for a boy about his age?" their dad asked, pointing to Christopher.

"How old is he?" the salesman asked, snapping his gum as he talked.

Their dad frowned and looked back at Christopher. "I dunno. How old are you?"

"He's eleven." Emily sounded as if she were throwing the words out. Then she turned around and sauntered off to another section of the store.

Their dad watched her go, and Sam was surprised to see that he looked a bit hurt. Sam even felt a bit sorry for him.

But then he flashed a cocky grin at the salesman, and the moment was gone. "What's the latest and greatest for an eleven-year-old boy?"

"PS5? Nintendo Switch? Luna?" Each of the guy's suggestions was punctuated with a snap of his gum. He was starting to annoy Sam. He could do a better sales job than this guy was doing. At least he'd try to be a bit more polite.

Their dad shrugged and looked at Sam. "What do you figure?"

The next few minutes were taken up with discussing the various aspects of the choices available. While they talked, Christopher's eyes got bigger and bigger.

Sam knew they wouldn't be able to get anything that needed to be hooked up to the television, so they settled on a Nintendo.

"Can I get the blue one?" Christopher asked, just staring at the box.

"You can get whatever color you want. And you can pick out some games for it too."

Christopher just stood there, his mouth open in disbelief. Though he already had a Nintendo, it was older and secondhand. Sam knew his little brother had wanted a brand-new Nintendo Switch ever since he'd seen one of his friends with one, but he also knew it would take Christopher years to save up for one on the allowance he got.

But at the same time, Sam wasn't so sure Grandma or Grandpa would think it was such a good idea.

"Are you sure you should spend so much money?" Sam asked.

Their dad shot Sam a frown and then patted Christopher on the shoulder. "Nothing's too good for my little guy."

The grin on Christopher's face erased any concerns Sam might have.

"So, what kind of games do you want?"

Christopher looked at Sam, not sure what to do.

"Go ahead, buddy," Sam said, grinning at his little brother, happy to see the smile on Christopher's face.

While Christopher and their dad were deciding on games, Sam went to find his sister. She was just wandering around, her hands in her pockets, looking grouchy.

"What's your deal?" he hissed, grabbing her by the arm. "Why are you acting like such a jerk?"

Emily glared at him. "What's yours? I thought you were so ticked at him and now you're acting like he's your best friend."

"Hardly." Sam glanced back to where their dad and Christopher were still busy trying to decide on games.

Christopher looked thrilled. "I've only been talking to him because you're not."

Emily shrugged and wandered down another aisle. "I don't know what to say."

"Well, neither do I. You could help me out a bit."

Sam didn't mean to sound so mad, but he didn't know what to think either.

She picked up a box and then put it back. Next, she picked up a camera and pretended to take Sam's picture. "I just don't know about all of this. We don't see him for years, and all of a sudden he's here buying presents." She put the camera down and picked up another one. "Seems weird."

"It is weird. But it could be fun."

"I guess." But Emily didn't sound convinced.

"So here's where you two are. Did you find what you wanted?" Their dad glanced at the camera Emily had in her hand. "That's pretty cool. Digital camera? Do you have one?"

"No." Emily quickly put it down and shoved her hands in her back pockets.

"Really? Your grandparents haven't sprung for a camera for you yet?"

"Well, they don't exactly have a ton of money."

Their dad waved his hand as if this were unimportant. "Don't need a ton of money to buy your own kid a digital camera." He picked one up. "Would you like this one?"

Emily's eyes got huge as she glanced at the shiny pink camera their dad was holding. "That's a pretty cool one," she admitted.

"This would be a good one. Small enough to fit in your

purse, but has lots of megapixels and a nice zoom." Kevin glanced around, and the gum-snapping employee was right there.

Knew a good customer when he saw one, Sam figured. Maybe the kid wasn't so dumb after all.

"I'd like this one. In pink. We should get a case for it too and an extra memory card. And an extra battery." Their dad flashed a quick grin at Emily. "Always good to have a spare."

Sam could see Emily felt overwhelmed by this, and, truth to tell, so was he.

"And while we're getting this together, Sam, you should figure out what you want," their dad was saying.

"Sam always said he wanted an iPod Touch," Christopher put in.

"Well, that's a great present," their dad said. "Why don't you get us one of those too?" he said to the salesman before Sam could protest. Even though he'd always wanted one, as Christopher had said, an iPod Touch seemed too much from someone who was almost a stranger to him.

But off the sales guy scurried, only too glad to add to their selections.

A few minutes later, Sam held a cellophane-wrapped box in his hands. In spite of his reservations he couldn't help but enjoy the feel of it, the promise of the picture on the front of the box. Brand spanking new.

"Is that the kind you wanted, big guy?" his dad asked, looking over his shoulder.

"Well, I dunno." Sam felt confused. He didn't want to look greedy and yet... "It's kind of expensive." Sam felt like he had to at least make some protest.

"No problem. Nothing's too much for my kids. I think

we should get a case for it too, though, and some wireless earbuds. And grab a bluetooth speaker." And off they went again.

A few minutes later the sales guy was ringing everything up, and for just a moment, Sam thought his dad was going to change his mind. Tell them it was all just a joke.

But no, everything got bagged and handed over the counter to their dad.

"Here you go, kids," he said, handing out their purchases. "Think of this as a pre-Christmas gift. A warm-up."

Sam took the crinkly bag, full of... stuff. Pre-Christmas gifts? A warm-up? Surely he wasn't going to get them more?

And sneaking behind that question was one that had been growing the whole time they'd been picking things out: What would Grandma and Grandpa think?

"Anything else you want to do?" their dad was asking them. "We've still got time. Any other Christmas shopping you want to take care of?"

"I have some other shopping to do," Emily said, her voice all funny and quiet, and Sam didn't blame her. A digital camera. He knew she'd been saving up for one, but it would have taken her forever to get all that money together. "I wouldn't mind checking a few things out. I'd like to head out on my own though."

"We need to pick a place to meet," Sam said.

"One hour? The candy stand by the food court?" Emily said.

"Okay. As long as one of you boys knows where to go," their dad said, glancing from Sam to Christopher. That meant they would be staying with their dad.

"Do you need to do any Christmas shopping, guys?" their dad asked.

"I want to look at some magazines," Christopher said. "For building a house."

Their dad ruffled Christopher's short hair. "You planning on building your own place?"

Christopher just laughed at his dad's little joke. "No. I want to get some ideas for a house for Uncle Pete and Aunt Dana. They're getting married, and I said I would help them plan their house."

"You're a smart guy," their dad said, sounding like he was really impressed. "I didn't know I had such a smart son."

Christopher was just lapping it up, which, for some reason he couldn't quite figure out, kind of annoyed Sam.

"Sam, what about you?"

Sam shrugged. "Yeah, I need to find something for my girlfriend."

"Do you want some help?"

"Well, I guess." He still felt funny around his dad and was a bit jealous of Emily, being out in the mall on her own while he was stuck with their dad and Christopher.

They walked around the mall. Once his dad found out that he was looking for a present for Arielle, he had all kinds of suggestions, none of which Sam could afford.

"I can help you out with buying it," his dad said. "I don't mind pitching in some money."

Sam stopped looking at a bracelet after he turned over the white tag that had the price written on it. "No. I should buy it myself."

"Hey, if you want to put a sparkle in your special girl's life, you need to buy something sparkly."

Sam wondered if their dad had ever bought something sparkly for their mother. Or if he had ever bought a present for that other woman he'd been living with awhile back.

But he kept his thoughts to himself. He'd just gotten a big present from him; he could hardly get snarky on his dad now.

"I'll think of something," Sam said, turning away from the jewelry store.

They stopped at a bookstore, and their dad insisted on buying some house-plan magazines for Christopher, who was just beaming. As they walked down the mall, still looking for something for Arielle, Sam saw that Christopher was looking up at his dad as if he were his new hero.

That bugged him a bit, but what could he say?

Nothing, it turned out. As they shopped and wandered aimlessly, Sam couldn't think of a thing to say to the man who had been such an obsession to him for so long.

Turned out he didn't have to say much anyway.

Christopher was a regular motor mouth. He had asked their dad a ton of questions about his work—construction on overseas projects. And where he lived—in camps and hotels. And his truck—leased. Sam just wandered along behind them, listening.

"I still say you should let me help you out with the gift for your honey," his dad said as they walked toward the candy stand to meet up with Emily. "You want to make a good impression on her if you want to keep her."

Sam felt a bit confused by his father. On the one hand he seemed full of advice on how to treat a girlfriend, but on the other, he hadn't been much of a husband.

Sam was getting tired just trying to sort it all out.

They found Emily waiting at an empty table in the food court, texting on her phone. She had a couple of bags on the table, which she pushed down onto the floor as soon as she saw them.

"Hey," she said as they came nearer. "I'm done."

"We are too," Sam said.

There was an awkward moment as they kind of looked at each other.

"Look what Dad got me," Christopher said, pulling the magazines out of the bag. "Now I can make up some really good plans for Uncle Pete and Aunt Dana."

"Awesome," Emily said, giving Christopher a tight little smile, which disappeared as quickly as it had come.

"I guess we should probably get back to the farm," Emily said.

"You guys don't want any candy? Ice cream? We didn't have dessert at the restaurant." Their dad was pulling out his wallet again.

The magic bullet, Sam thought. But Christopher seemed game and walked over to the bins of the candy store, looking them over with bright eyes.

Sam and Emily both said no as their dad went over to Christopher and helped him pick out a bunch of treats.

"He's going to get sick eating all that candy," Emily said.

Sam didn't want to say anything. His head felt tired. He just wanted to go home.

"Are you downloading your songs right away?" Emily asked.

"You can get your camera set up on the computer first."

Emily gave him a funny look. "I thought I'd have to fight you for that."

Christopher came back, eyes bright, bag full of candy. "I got something for everyone," he said. "And you have to wait until Christmas to get it."

"He's a generous little kid, my boy is," their dad said, rubbing Christopher's head.

My boy? Was Christopher their dad's boy a couple of months ago? A couple of years ago? Sam thought as he started walking toward the mall entrance. Suddenly, more than anything, he just wanted to get home.

The drive back was as quiet as the drive to the mall had been. Emily stared out the window. Christopher looked tired, and Sam, well, he was still at a loss for conversation.

Their dad stopped his rig in front of the house and put the gearshift in park. "I guess this is good-bye until we see each other again."

"You're not coming in the house?" Christopher asked, gathering up the bags holding the presents their dad had bought him.

"No. I'd better just lay low awhile, sport." Their dad rubbed Christopher's head again, grinning at him. "You make sure you get to bed on time."

He leaned over the seat to look at Emily and Sam, sitting in the back. "If you need any ideas for your girl, be glad to help." He handed Sam, Emily, and Christopher each a business card. "My cell phone number," he explained. "Call me anytime you want. If you want to talk or if you need anything. Just call. I'm around until after Christmas."

Sam pocketed the card. So easy. For years nothing from their dad; now they had an instant connection to him day and night. If they wanted one.

"Thanks for the... present," Sam said, holding up the bag. The crinkling of the plastic made him feel a bit guilty, and he wondered what Grandma and Grandpa would say when they saw what the kids had gotten.

Well, what could they say? he thought. This was their dad, and he wanted to buy them something.

"You all take care. And make sure you call me. Anytime. I'll be in touch with Charlotte and Bob to let them know when I'll be coming for you guys again."

Sam just nodded as he slipped out of the truck.

A sudden gust of winter wind sliced through his open coat, and he pulled it close, shivering. He helped Christopher out of the huge truck and shut the door.

And then their dad was gone.

The taillights of his big truck winked through the exhaust plume as he braked and then turned down the drive to the road.

"So. That was fun." Emily sounded kind of sarcastic, but Sam knew how she felt. The whole situation felt weird. And he didn't know what to think of it all.

"Well, we got some nice stuff out of the deal," Sam said, trying to sound like it mattered.

Trouble was, it didn't.

Chapter Eleven

"Hey, Grandpa," Emily said, dropping her bag on the floor in the hallway. "Where's Grandma?"

Grandpa looked up from his television show. "Oh, hey kids. How was dinner?"

Emily glanced at Sam, who shrugged. Christopher was dumping the contents of his bag on the kitchen table, his eyes shining.

"Very fancy," Emily said. "Tasted good."

"Where did you go?" Grandpa hit MUTE on the television and got out of his recliner.

Emily glanced at the bag she had put around the corner and hoped he wouldn't notice. She still felt weird about the camera.

"I don't remember the name of the place, but I know the food was expensive," Sam said.

"They had a cart full of desserts, but my stomach hurt so I didn't get any." Christopher ripped open the top of his Nintendo box like he couldn't get into it fast enough.

"Grandma left to take Madison and Jennifer to Mrs. Adlai's place," Grandpa was saying. He glanced over at the kitchen table. "Whatcha got there, Christopher?"

"A Nintendo Switch," Christopher said, his voice full of awe.

"What's that?" Grandpa frowned, picking up the instruction booklet.

"It's for playing video games." Christopher tugged at the heavy plastic, trying to get it out of the packaging.

"Here, let me help you with that." Grandpa got out a knife and started carefully cutting away the hard plastic shell surrounding the Nintendo.

"When will Grandma be back?" Emily asked.

"She left about twenty minutes ago. She hoped to see you kids before she left." Grandpa gave her a quick smile. "What did Kevin get you?"

"Sam got an iPod Touch."

Grandpa frowned. "Well, I suppose that means something to you," he said.

Emily had to smile. Good ol' Grandpa. In a way she was lucky he didn't know that much about the latest gadgets. He wouldn't know how much Sam's iPod had cost.

"I got a camera."

"Really?" Grandpa's eyebrows lifted in surprise, but before he could quiz her about it, she grabbed the bag. "I'm going upstairs," she said. "Gotta make a call."

Once she got to her room, she grabbed her phone and scanned the screen for new messages. But there was no call from Ashley.

She must've sent her friend at least a half-dozen text messages already, but Ashley hadn't replied to any of them. Emily felt her heart sink. When Ashley had first started dating Ryan she'd ignored Emily as well, but Emily thought her friend was over that weirdness.

But now Ashley was ignoring her again.

Boyfriends. Who needed them? Emily thought.

But in the meantime she needed to talk to someone. She didn't know what to think about the shopping trip with her dad. She'd dreamed of having her own digital camera, but it was taking her a long time to save up for one. Aunt Rosemary had given her a cool old film camera, but digital was what she had really wanted.

Trouble was, now she felt guilty about getting it from her dad. Like she hadn't earned it or deserved it.

She should never have let her dad buy her such an expensive present. She corrected herself: pre-Christmas present. If that was just a warm-up, as he had said, what would the actual Christmas present be like?

She rubbed her forehead, hoping she would have a chance to talk to Ashley tomorrow. She really needed to get Ashley's take on their dad's sudden appearance in their lives and how Emily felt about the invasion.

Because she wasn't sure herself what to think.

Okay, enough about her dad, she thought, pushing herself off her bed. Time to think about something else.

She found the magazines she had gotten from the library and leaned back against her headboard, flipping through the copious amounts of ads that took up more than half the pages in the magazines.

She found a picture of a star who had just gotten married. The actress was looking over her shoulder, dressed in a frothy wedding gown, laughing up at the camera like everything was all wonderful in her life, her handsome husband smiling at her in the background.

The star looked like her mother, Emily thought, touching her face. And then Emily's mind slipped back to her mom's diary that Emily had found awhile back.

Her mother didn't have a fancy wedding with a pretty dress and bridesmaids all dressed up. Had she regretted that? Had she wished she'd waited? Had their dad pushed her to make a quick decision?

Emily stared at the picture and tried to think what her mother would have looked like in this dress. What her father would have looked like standing beside her in a tuxedo.

Then she blinked, and panic slivered through her.

While she could easily imagine the smiling groom as her father, when she tried to picture her mother as the bride, all she got was wavery features that didn't come together.

Emily pushed the magazine aside, dug out her photo albums, and flipped through the pages. But because her mom had always been the one to snap the pictures, there were few photos of her. When Emily finally found one, she felt as if she were looking at a stranger.

She bit her lip, somehow feeling disloyal. And behind that feeling came a burst of anger. Her mother was dead. And their father, who hadn't even seemed to care about them until now, was alive.

It wasn't fair, and it wasn't right.

And now he was back, trying to make up for the lost years. As if he could. As if buying them things would make up for all the time he was gone. If he hadn't left, maybe their mother would still be alive. If he had stayed, they would still be a family.

Emily snapped the photo album shut and pushed the magazines aside. Right now she had too many things on her mind and too few people to talk to about them.

Suddenly there was a knock on her door, and then her grandmother was looking into the room.

"How are you, honey? How was your visit with your father?"

Emily glanced over at the camera, still in the plastic-wrapped box, sitting on her chair. Grandma followed the direction of her gaze and frowned.

"Is this new?"

Emily sighed. "Yeah. Dad got it for me. A pre-Christmas present, he said."

"Well, that's nice." But Emily could tell from the tone in Grandma's voice that she didn't really think it was that nice at all. "I'm curious what he's going to get you for Christmas if that's a pre-Christmas present."

Though Grandma was trying to sound lighthearted, Emily could tell she wasn't really happy about it.

Emily let out a sigh.

"What's the matter, honey?" Grandma asked, coming a little farther into the room.

Emily hugged her knees, not sure she wanted to talk to Grandma about her father.

"Nothing," Emily said, giving her grandma a forced smile.

Grandma smoothed a strand of hair back from her face, looking as if she didn't quite believe Emily was telling her the truth and wanting to comfort her somehow. "If you want to talk about something, I'm available," she said.

"Thanks, Grandma." Emily gave her a quick smile, but as Grandma left the room, Emily didn't think she could ever talk to her about her father. She knew Grandma and Grandpa didn't like him all that much.

Only Ashley would truly understand how weird everything was for her, she thought.

But Ashley was doing her own thing. With her own boyfriend.

THE BELL RANG, signaling the end of the period. Emily gathered her books and headed out of the classroom. She hadn't seen Ashley on the bus, nor had she caught her at her locker before school. It was as if her friend had disappeared.

She hoped she'd see Ashley at lunchtime, she thought, hurrying to her locker.

Just as she snapped the combination lock shut, she heard someone call her name.

It was Miss Simons, coming down the hall toward her.

"Emily, do you have a minute?" she asked, walking up to her. "I was hoping to have a word with you."

Emily felt her stomach flip over slowly. From the serious look on her face and the way she was talking, Emily guessed Miss Simons wanted to talk about their dad. She wasn't sure she wanted to. She didn't know what to think about him right now, and she certainly didn't know what to tell anyone else.

Emily took a small step to the side. Just a tiny hint that she was in a bit of a hurry. She wanted to catch Ashley.

Then Miss Simons gave Emily a careful smile. And Emily knew what was coming.

"I also want to see how you're doing," Miss Simons said, her eyes holding Emily's.

Emily did so not want to talk about her father at this moment!

"This must be difficult," Miss Simons said, keeping her voice low so the kids walking past them couldn't hear. "Do you want to come to my room and talk about anything?"

Emily liked Miss Simons and was super excited she was going to be her aunt, but in the school she was a teacher and Emily was a pupil. And crossing those lines made things awkward.

"Maybe some other time?" Emily said.

Miss Simons nodded. Like she knew.

"Of course. I'll see you soon."

Emily gave her an apologetic smile and took another step away. "Sorry, I gotta run," she said. "I gotta catch Ashley."

"Sure. You take care." Miss Simons gave her another quick smile, and then she was gone.

Emily slung her backpack over her shoulder and walked down the hall.

She found Ashley in the cafeteria, sitting with Ryan.

Of course.

Today Ashley wore bright lipstick and too much eyeliner, and she was acting all flirty. She looked as if she'd been taken over by aliens. Ashley was laughing at something Ryan was saying, but it was kind of a fake laugh.

She's trying too hard, Emily thought. She sighed inwardly, remembering their usual lunches.

Emily sat down beside her, and Ashley gave her a quick smile.

"Hey, Em. How's it going?" Ashley asked, giggling.

"Did you get any of my text messages?" Emily asked.

Ashley gave her a goofy pout and then waved her fingers, flashing bright red nail polish, another departure from her usual light-colored polish. "Oh, those. Sorry. I didn't have a chance to answer. Been really, really busy and all."

With what? Emily wanted to ask. But as she looked across the table, she figured it had something to do with Ryan.

He swirled his french fries through his ketchup, looking kind of bored. Like he wasn't even that interested in Ashley. Was something up with them? Was that why Ashley was acting so strange?

"Your text said your dad came back." Ashley twirled a piece of hair around her finger. "What's that like?"

"It's, well, different." Emily glanced across the table toward Ryan, wishing he wasn't around so she could have some face time with her friend.

She was about to tell Ashley about her shopping trip with her father when her friend glanced across the table and tapped Ryan on the arm.

"Are we still heading out this weekend with your sister?"

He looked up, nodded and then turned his attention back to his fries. He seemed mesmerized by them.

And when Emily saw the disappointment on her friend's face, she wanted to kick Ryan. Ashley was a great girl. How come he was treating her so badly?

"Or we could just hang at your house with your sister,"

Ashley said. "Watch that new movie that my mom bought me."

Ryan shrugged. "Yeah. Sure. Whatever."

Her bright red lips made the hard set of Ashley's mouth difficult to miss. But then she got her smile back in place before she turned to Emily. "Anything new with you?"

"I got a new camera from my dad." She had a sudden inspiration. "You want to come over and help me figure it out?"

Ashley bit her lip, looking back at Ryan as if she needed his permission. "I'm not sure." She waited a second, hoping Ryan would come up with some excuse for her. "I think I'll be busy."

Emily felt a moment of panic. Was this what it would be like from now on, Ashley constantly waiting to see if Ryan was doing something before deciding if she was available for Emily?

She gave Ashley a wan smile and then got up. "Let me know if you change your mind, okay?" She glanced from Ashley to Ryan, who was still staring at his french fries.

What a loser. What did Ashley see in him anyway?

She turned and walked out of the cafeteria, wishing she didn't feel like crying.

"DID YOU FIGURE OUT what to get Arielle yet?"

Sam looked up from his locker at his friend Jake, who was leaning with one shoulder against the lockers, his hands shoved in the front pocket of his blue-and-white-checked hoodie.

He had the hood up, covering his dark hair.

"You having a bad hair day?" Sam joked, flicking one finger at the strings of his friend's hoodie.

"I'm in disguise," Jake said, glancing around. "You know that chick in our bio class? The one that keeps scoping me out?"

"Trish Nelson?"

"Yeah. Well, she tried to ask me out on a date." Jake rolled his eyes.

"I think you should go for it," Sam joked, closing the door of his locker.

"Dude, that's wrong on so many levels." Jake shuddered. "She's a cheerleader. I mean, how lame is that?"

"From what I've seen during their practices, cheerleaders are far from lame," Sam said with a grin. "And she's kind of cute."

"I'll tell Arielle you said that." Jake glanced around before he pushed himself away from the locker.

"As for Arielle's present," Sam continued, "funds are limited so there's not much to pick from in my price range."

"You seriously need to find a job that makes you more money than that airport job does," Jake said. "Did you ever get your car fixed?"

"Not yet. It needs more than I can afford right now, and I want to get something really nice for Arielle for Christmas."

"See, and that's why I'm avoiding Miss Cheerful Cheerleader," Jake said. "Women make life too complicated." He grinned, looking over Sam's shoulder. "And speaking of complications, here comes yours. I'm gone." Jake tossed off a wave. "See ya at noon."

Jake gave Arielle a quick nod as they passed each other.

"Hey, good to see you," Sam said giving her a smile.

Arielle had her hair loose today, just the way Sam liked it. She wasn't the type to wear much makeup, but then, she didn't need to. She was pretty enough without it.

"Hey yourself." She gave him a careful smile, and Sam guessed from the sympathetic look on her face what she was going to say next. "I heard about your dad coming back."

"Guess there are no secrets in this town," Sam said with a bit of a laugh, though it did bug him a bit. Back in San Diego, his life outside of school was his own. Lots of his friends didn't even know where he lived, which was okay with him most of the time.

Here, not only did they know where he lived and what kind of farm they had, but it also seemed like they knew a million little details about his life and his family. Sometimes, if Christopher was especially chatty on the bus, they even knew what kind of cereal Sam had eaten that morning.

"How is that for you?" Arielle continued.

Sam sighed. "Not sure I want to talk about it yet."

Thankfully she got the hint. Arielle was smart that way. "Okay, then how about college? Got your application forms out yet?" Arielle asked, pulling her books closer to her chest. She gave Sam a shy smile as they walked down the crowded hall of the school, but he couldn't smile back.

He wasn't sure if he wanted to go there either.

"Not yet." He didn't want to tell his girlfriend that he hadn't even filled them out yet.

"Time is ticking," Arielle added.

"I'll get them out on time." Sam didn't mean to snap the

words out, but he couldn't help it. "I have a lot on my mind lately." Then he sighed. "I'm sorry. It's just, with my dad and all . . ."

"I figured that might be a problem for you." Arielle touched his arm, and Sam was glad for the small connection.

"I just don't understand why he's even bothered to come back after all this time." Sam shoved his hands in his pockets as they headed toward the cafeteria, his frustration spilling out in spite of not wanting to talk about it a few moments earlier. "He's messing up my mind. And even worse, he's messing up Christopher's mind. The poor kid already thinks Dad left us because of him. For a while he was convinced that Dad was coming back here, and he was going to take just me and Emily with him. Now Dad is all over him, acting like Christopher is the best thing since sliced bread. And because he hasn't had much attention from Dad, Christopher is lapping it all up."

Sam shot a quick glance at Arielle. "Sorry for dumping all this on you. Guess I did want to talk about it after all. I'm just so frustrated I don't know what to do."

"I wish I could help you," she said. "I can't imagine what that must be like for you and Emily and Christopher."

"I've been waiting for years to talk to him. To ask him why he left. To ask him a ton of questions—and then he shows up, and all he wants to do is buy us stuff and help me buy—" He stopped himself before he said "your present." Because that would really make him look pathetic.

"You know what they say about money," Arielle said, nudging him with her elbow. "It can't buy love."

Sam shook his head. "My dad sure seems to be trying."

They walked in silence through the noisy crowds of the

hallways. Then Arielle spoke up. "Well you can't let him interfere with your plans for your future."

"So we're back to those college application forms?"

"If you don't fill them out, you'll miss out."

"I'll get them done."

"When?" Arielle prompted.

Sam's simmering frustration overflowed. "You know, that's so easy for you." Sam stopped and turned to her, trying to hold back. "Your life has always been so normal. So easy. Your mom and dad live together. Your dad has a steady job—town cop, no less. You live in the same place you've always lived, the same house. I've had to move because my mother died. I've had to change my friends, change my school, get used to this lousy cold weather. Sometimes I still feel like I'm catching up. How am I supposed to know what to do with my future, when my past is such a mess? I feel like my life is spinning out of control."

He caught himself, realizing he was raising his voice. "I'm sorry," he muttered. "I just feel like the past few days have been crazy, and I don't know where my feet are going to land."

Arielle just smiled at him and then squeezed his arm. "Maybe making your own decisions about your future is a way to get control back. Decide for yourself where your feet are going to end up." She spoke softly, but her words hit home.

He nodded. "I suppose you're right. I was hoping to fill them in online, but Grandma said she wanted me to fill out the actual papers. Said that way she can look over them to make sure I haven't made any mistakes."

"That's not such a bad idea."

"You agree with my grandma." Sam scratched his head, feeling cornered.

"I think your grandma cares enough about you to make sure you don't have to do more work than necessary," Arielle said, flashing him a quick grin. She added a toss of her hair, like she was flirting with him. "And I don't mind having a look at them either, if you want."

"Great, now I've got two women who want to have a hand in my future," Sam said, pretending he was joking when, in fact, he was feeling the extra pressure.

Just as they turned the corner to the cafeteria, they nearly bumped into Emily, who came charging through the doors.

"Hey, what's up?" Sam said, stepping aside just in time.

Emily looked at him and then at Arielle, her eyes snapping. She was ticked off. She waved her hand at both of them. "Nothing. Everything's just fine." But she sounded sarcastic. Then she took off down the hallway, brushing past people as if she didn't even see them.

"I wonder what was bothering her," Arielle said. "She looked upset."

"Emily's always upset. It's her default mood."

Arielle frowned, like she didn't get it.

Sam held open the door for Arielle. "I wouldn't worry about it. Whatever got her in a snit, she'll forget about it soon enough."

He knew the comment was petty, but he was feeling a bit like Emily himself lately. And he wasn't sure what to do about it. He didn't think Arielle would understand.

Besides, he still had to get some kind of clue of what to get her for Christmas.

Chapter Twelve

"You make sure you get your homework done," Sam said, standing over Christopher. "Grandma said I was in charge while she's at Bedford Gardens, and I'm making sure you get it done."

"I didn't hear Grandma say you were in charge," Christopher said. He just had one more level to go on the new Nintendo Switch, and he would beat his high score. Of course he only had five high scores. He hadn't been playing this game that long.

"Grandpa said it too."

"Where is Grandpa anyway?"

"Having coffee with his buddies at AA Tractor. And he told me the same thing." Sam nudged Christopher with the toe of his sock.

"Eeuw," Christopher said, pulling his leg back. "Don't touch me with your stinky sock."

"I'll touch you all I want," Sam said, poking him again. Then again. "I'll touch you until you let me play with your Nintendo."

He poked Christopher again, causing him to miss a jump, and suddenly the game he was playing was over.

"Sam, stop it," Christopher snapped. "You made me lose the game."

"Good. Then you can get back to your homework," Sam said, bending over to take the Nintendo away.

"And you should be working on your college stuff," Christopher said, getting up.

"You take care of your homework, and I'll take care of my own stuff," Sam said. He sounded mad, but Christopher didn't care. Ever since their dad had taken them out for dinner and bought them stuff afterward, everyone seemed to be kind of snappy. Even Grandma sounded a bit mad when he tried to show her all the games their dad had gotten him for the Nintendo.

"Hello," a lady's voice hollered from the porch.

It was Miss Simons. At least she would be fun to have around, Christopher thought.

"Dana. Hey." Uncle Pete got up from his chair, a goofy smile on his face.

Emily was up in her room, which was fine with Christopher. She'd been really grumpy since Sunday too, and Christopher just didn't get it. She'd been talking about getting a digital camera for months, and now she had one and she hadn't taken any pictures. She hadn't even taken it out of the box.

Miss Simons came into the house, unwrapping a scarf from around her neck. Her cheeks were bright red and her smile was wide. Uncle Pete gave her a quick kiss, and that made her smile even more.

"Hey, beautiful," Uncle Pete said to her. "How's it going?"

"I went to visit a florist after school today and we got some great ideas for flowers." She had a bunch of papers in her hand, which reminded Christopher of the house plans he had been working on.

He ran upstairs and gathered up some of the sketches. When he came back downstairs, Miss Simons stood in the living room, the lights of the Christmas tree making her glow red, blue, yellow, and green.

"Wow, that tree looks stunning," she said.

"Every year I think that tree is the best, and I have to say it, this one is just beautiful," Pete was saying.

Christopher thought it would have looked nicer with a popcorn string on it, but no one else agreed with him. It still bugged him that Emily had just thrown all his hard work out, like it didn't matter.

Miss Simons, or Aunt Dana as Uncle Pete kept saying they should call her, at least when they weren't at school, was so nice to everyone. Christopher was excited to think that she was going to be their aunt and live on the farm. And he was excited to show them the plans he'd put together.

"What have you got there, Christopher?" Miss Simons asked, turning around to look at him.

Christopher looked down at the stack of magazines and papers he held. "Some ideas for your and Uncle Pete's new house."

"New house? Well, that sounds interesting."

"Christopher has just been goofing around with some ideas," Uncle Pete said. "I don't know if we can really do anything yet."

"You can look at my plans," Christopher said.

"Why don't we do that?" Pete said, pulling up a chair.

"This was the first one I did," Christopher said, showing Uncle Pete the plan he put together before he had the magazines to work with.

Aunt Dana sat down beside Uncle Pete. "You drew these out? Wow, they're pretty good."

Dana picked up one of the magazines that Christopher had gotten from his dad. "Seven energy-efficient homes," she read aloud. "That sounds interesting."

"I read that if you put in solar panels you can save a lot of money on your electricity."

"But solar panels cost a lot of money to buy," Pete said, flipping through the magazine.

"But you could save the money you spend on them in lower electricity bills."

"You've put some thought into this, Christopher," Aunt Dana said, putting the magazine down.

"And you've been studying the advertising," Uncle Pete said with a grin. "Tell us about this plan."

Christopher turned the paper toward them both. "This was my first idea."

Uncle Pete nodded as he looked it over. "Looks like you put the rooms all in a row. Like a long, skinny rectangle."

"The magazine says that if you put most of the windows facing south, you'll get extra heat in the house, and if you make the walls extra thick you can retain heat."

"This one is kind of neat," Uncle Pete said, showing it to Aunt Dana.

"I love it. It's a great plan," she said.

Christopher felt a flush of pride, glad that he had done the extra work—and really glad that his dad had bought him the magazines. "Here's another one," he said, grabbing another piece of paper.

"This one seems a bit small," Uncle Pete said, picking up the plan. "But I like the idea."

Miss Simons moved a bit closer. "I really like having the kitchen closer to the dining room."

"How about we draw this one a bit bigger?" Uncle Pete asked. "Maybe move the kitchen."

Christopher was getting more excited. "I can do that," he said, flipping through his stuff for some blank paper. But he had used up all that he had.

He looked into the kitchen and saw a pile of blank paper stacked in one corner. He pulled one sheet off the stack, grabbed his ruler and pen, and made a bigger square on the back of the paper. "Oops. This is crooked. I'll do another one." He grabbed another sheet of paper.

"Shouldn't you use a pencil?" Uncle Pete asked.

"Couldn't find one." This time Christopher drew more carefully. "There's more paper if this doesn't work."

He finished the square and grinned up at Uncle Pete. "Where should we put the kitchen?"

"That would be Dana's call," Uncle Pete said.

Miss Simons pointed with her pen. "How about here?"

Uncle Pete made another suggestion, and soon they were busy drawing up more plans. Good thing there was lots of paper.

"I don't know. I'm still thinking I'd like a bigger dining room," Uncle Pete said.

"I had another plan," Christopher said, suddenly remembering. "I think it's upstairs. I'll go get it."

"You do that," Uncle Pete said, giving him a quick smile, and Christopher scampered upstairs, happy to be helping.

He got to the landing, and because he was looking so closely at his papers, he tripped and they fell out of his hands. As he was picking them up, he heard Uncle Pete talking to Miss Simons. They were using their grown-up voices.

And they were talking about his dad.

"The poor kids are so mixed up now that he's back," Uncle Pete was saying. He sounded angry.

"I don't blame them. This has got to be a huge upheaval for them. Did he give anyone any warning?"

"Nope. Just showed up out of the blue, throwing money around like he's some kind of oil baron. Mom and Dad have been trying to see what he's up to."

Christopher rearranged his papers, his ears burning. Uncle Pete didn't sound like he liked his dad at all. And what did he mean, calling his dad an oil baron? It didn't sound nice.

Miss Simons sighed. "Those poor kids. I'm glad you told me."

"Figured you needed to know. That's why I'm putting up with Christopher and this house-plan thing. Humoring him. So play along. It's not like we're doing any of it. I mean, solar panels? Like I can afford that." Uncle Pete sounded like he was laughing—laughing at him. "But it helps keep his mind off his dad."

Christopher looked down at the papers in his hand. This was a waste of his time. He was about to continue up the stairs to his bedroom when he heard Uncle Pete call his name.

He had to keep going now.

"There you are," Uncle Pete said when Christopher came down the hallway toward the living room. "Let's see what you've got."

Then the phone rang, and Uncle Pete held up his hand to Christopher, telling him to wait a minute as he answered the phone.

"Hey, Brad. Yeah, I got a couple of minutes."

Christopher walked to the kitchen table and sat down, looking over the papers. He wasn't excited anymore at all.

"Whatcha doin, buddy?" Sam dropped onto an empty chair across the table from him.

"Nothin'," Christopher said, pushing the papers around.

Sam picked up the last plan Christopher had made. "Well, you're getting good at making squares," he teased.

Christopher didn't answer. He was sick of getting teased. Sick of being treated like he was a little kid.

Then Sam frowned and grabbed another plan. "Where did you get the paper for all of this?" Sam's voice sounded hard. He was flipping hurriedly through the last plans Christopher had drawn up, his eyebrows pulled together like he did when he was mad.

And Christopher knew he'd done something wrong.

"I got the paper from the stack . . . over there." He pointed with his pen. "On the corner of the table. I thought it was leftover paper from Grandma and Grandpa doing the books." Sometimes if they made mistakes printing things out, Grandma would let Christopher use the other side of the paper they used to draw on.

Sam put down the page he was holding and marched over to the pile of paper, picked it up, and turned it over.

The paper had printing on the front.

"I just used the empty back," Christopher said.

Sam shook the papers at Christopher. "What were you thinking? These are my college application forms and my forms for applying for student aid."

Christopher swallowed and looked down at the paper he was drawing on right now. Slowly he turned it over. And this time he paid closer attention to what was on it.

Across the top was printed the name of a college. Below that was a bunch of squares with words underneath. Some of the squares had been filled in with a pencil in Sam's printing.

"I can't send these away," Sam said, digging through the rest of Christopher's papers and flipping them over. "You used a whole bunch of my forms."

Christopher felt his stomach start to hurt again. He put his pen down and tried very hard not to get sad. He knew Sam would just get madder if he did.

"So, my man, sorry about the interruption. I had to talk to Brad about a problem I'm having with the tractor." Uncle Pete sat down and picked up one of the papers. "What do you have for me this time?"

Christopher couldn't say anything. He was trying too hard not to cry.

"Christopher? What's wrong?" Uncle Pete asked.

Sam threw down the papers and they fluttered over the table. "What's wrong is that Christopher just finished drawing all over my application forms."

"Just some of them," Christopher managed to say, hating how his voice sounded so small.

"Doesn't matter. They're ruined. You know how long it took me to work on these? How hard it was to get them? Now I'll never get them done in time."

Sam stomped down the hallway and up the stairs just as Emily and Dana came into the kitchen.

"What gives with Sam?" Emily asked as they joined Christopher and Pete at the table.

"He's ticked at Christopher for drawing on his college application forms." Pete patted Christopher on his shoulder. "You should have looked at them first, buddy."

Christopher swallowed and then swallowed again. He was doing everything wrong. Sam was mad at him, and Uncle Pete didn't really want to see his plans.

He got up from the table and ran upstairs. He jumped onto his bed and shoved his head under the pillow. He didn't want to talk to anyone, and he didn't want anyone to talk to him. He wasn't that important after all.

He stayed under the pillow for a while, but he could still hear Miss Simons and Emily talking downstairs.

Sam was probably playing with his Nintendo.

They weren't missing him one bit.

Christopher swiped his hands over his face and sat up. He wanted to talk to someone, but he didn't want to phone his friend Dylan Lonetree. Dylan had his own problems.

But who could he talk to?

Then he thought of the business card their dad had given them. He still had his in the pocket of his Sunday pants.

Christopher pulled himself out of the bed by his heels and dug in his pants pockets. Sure enough, there was the card. He snuck over to the spare room. Uncle Pete was staying in it now, and Christopher felt a little funny going in there, but he wanted to use the phone. Luckily it was on the cradle and not in Emily's room like it usually was.

He brought it back to his room, took a deep breath, and punched his dad's number into the handset.

It rang a bunch of times and just as Christopher was about to hang up, his dad answered.

"Dad?" Christopher said, trying to keep his voice quiet so they wouldn't hear him downstairs. "Are you there? This is Christopher."

"Hey, Chris. How are you doing? Where are you calling from?"

His dad sounded cheerful and really happy to hear from him, which made Christopher glad that he had called him.

"I'm at the farm. Where are you?"

"In my lonely old motel room. I miss you, sport."

He called him sport, like he was his buddy. Christopher smiled.

"I miss you too, Dad." Well, maybe he didn't miss him that much, but it seemed like something he should say back.

"You do? Hey, I'm glad we could spend some time together yesterday. Are you enjoying the Nintendo?"

"It's awesome. I play on it whenever I'm allowed." Christopher curled up on the bed, the phone pressed tight against his ear.

"You make sure you do your homework too, sport," his dad said.

"I do."

Then he didn't really know what to say.

"Are Sam and Emily there?" his dad asked.

"They're downstairs, talking to Uncle Pete and Aunt Dana. Well, she's not really our aunt yet, but when she marries Uncle Pete she will be."

"So your Uncle Pete is finally tying the knot. Good for him. She a nice person, or is she just after his money?"

"No. She's really nice," Christopher said, feeling a bit funny that his dad would say that about Miss Simons.

"Of course. I'm just kidding you. Say, are you into sports at all? Do you like playing hockey?"

"Uncle Pete just fixed up a snowmobile, and he said that someday, if he had time, he was going to make a skating rink on the yard. But sometimes, he said, we could just go skating on the lake. That would be fun. I've never been ice skating before."

"It's fun. I used to ice skate when I lived in Harding."

"Did you like it? Was it fun?" Christopher snuggled down even farther, happy that he had called his dad.

"Yeah, lots of fun. I'll have to see about taking you guys. Maybe we could do that next time. I'll do some phoning around. See what I can arrange."

Christopher just grinned. He and his dad were making plans and talking about things that Emily and Sam didn't know anything about.

"Did Sam and Emily have fun on Sunday?"

Christopher frowned. He didn't really want to talk about Sam and Emily with his dad, but he tried to remember some of the things they had said. "Sam said that we got some nice stuff out of the deal. And Emily was kind of quiet. They both liked supper though."

"Really." His dad was quiet for a moment, and Christopher wondered if maybe he had said something wrong.

"But I had fun. I still have a lot of the candy, and I'm going to make some boxes to put it in and give them to Grandma and Grandpa and Uncle Pete for Christmas presents."

"Say, while we're talking about Christmas, what do you want from me for Christmas?"

"But I already got a present," Christopher said.

"Like I said, that was just a warm-up. A pre-Christmas present. I haven't been around for a lot of Christmases, and I want to make it up to you and your brother and sister. And if you have any ideas for them, let me know."

Christopher frowned, trying to think. "I'd like a new bike, and I think Sam wants a snowboard. Emily always wants new clothes, but her clothes can be kind of strange so I don't know where you'd buy them." He thought a bit more. "But if I think of something else I can let you know."

"That'd be great."

In the background Christopher heard the sound of someone calling his dad's name. Sounded like a lady. "Do you have company?" Christopher asked.

"Just a friend who came to visit," his dad said, his voice quieter now. "She's about to leave."

"Who are you talking to?" The lady's voice grew louder.

Then it sounded like his dad put his hand over the phone because Christopher could only hear a little bit of what he was saying, and it was hard to understand.

Then he was back. "Sorry about that, sport. But I gotta go. And if you have any ideas about what you want, let me know. I've already written down what you told me."

"Okay. I'll try to think of something."

"And you can call me anytime, okay?"

Christopher smiled. "Okay."

"And tell your brother and sister that they can call me too," his dad added.

Christopher didn't know if he would. He kind of liked the idea that he was the only one talking to their dad.

"Take care, sport. Thanks a bunch for calling," his dad said.

"You're welcome."

Then his dad said good-bye, and that was the end of the conversation.

But Christopher held on to the phone for a few moments. At least his dad seemed happy to hear from him.

He didn't care what Sam and Emily said. He liked his dad. And he was going to call him again.

Chapter Thirteen

"Where are you headed?" Bob came into the porch from checking the cows, his hat crusted with the snow that was blowing around the corners of the farmhouse.

It was Wednesday morning, the children were long gone, and Charlotte had gotten most of her own work done.

"I need to do a few errands in town."

Bob frowned. "But weren't you there just the other day?"

"Yep. But now I need a few more groceries." And she needed to talk to Melody, but for some reason she didn't want to mention that to Bob. She didn't want to acknowledge that she was confused, frustrated, and afraid.

She wanted to pretend that everything was fine. As if Kevin was a mere blip in their life and that he would leave.

"You make sure you drive safe," Bob was saying. "The roads won't be drifting in yet, but by this afternoon, they could be."

The storm had blown in unexpectedly. Last night, she had paid extra attention to the forecast. The cheerful announcer had predicted sunshine and warmer temperatures.

Shows how much they know, Charlotte thought, wrapping her woolen scarf once more around her neck and tucking in the ends.

"Did you need me to pick up anything?" she asked, slipping her purse over the shoulder of her bulky coat.

Bob shook his head. "Pete went to town, you're going to town, I might go into town as well. Why don't we meet at Melody's for lunch?"

Looked like the whole Stevenson family would be in town today. However, she wasn't so sure she wanted to meet Bob at Melody's. She had hoped to sit with her friend over her lunch hour and get some much-needed advice. "Why don't we meet there at 12:30?" Melody's lunch break usually came before that, so she would have a chance to sit and chat before Bob came in.

Bob dropped a wet, cold kiss on her forehead, drew back, and gave her a quick smile. But in the lines bracketing his mouth and the worry in his eyes, she could see the same concerns that had awakened her at two this morning.

That had always been her worst time of the night. When the children were sick, 2:00 AM seemed to be when she would be walking the floors with them when they were babies, or soothing them when they were older.

After Denise had run away with Kevin at age eighteen, it was always at 2:00 AM that Charlotte would wake up from some disturbing dream, unable to sleep, worrying about her daughter and what would happen in her life.

And now, Kevin still haunted her sleep.

After an hour of praying, planning her day, and thinking

of the children, she had trudged to the family room, just off their bedroom, and sat in a chair, trying to read her Bible. Even then, her thoughts had spun around and around in worrisome circles.

What if Kevin was successful in getting the children?

What if the children didn't want to stay on the farm anymore?

What if everything turned into a long, drawn-out battle? Did she and Bob have the energy for that? Or, for that matter, the finances?

Pete needed a place to live. Sam was heading for college. The money simply wasn't there to do everything that needed to be done.

She had tried to pray, but her thoughts kept attacking her. She kept trying to think of ways to get around what Kevin wanted to do, but she couldn't come up with any. Finally, after an hour of more worry, she stumbled back to her bedroom and fell into a troubled sleep.

And now her head still felt fuzzy, so she didn't mind the bite of the cold air on her cheeks as she stepped outside. The blast of winter air invigorated her, and the squeak of the snow as she walked to her car made her feel suddenly more alive.

Her car protested being started in the cold weather, but in a few minutes it was warmed up, and Charlotte was headed off to town, snow swirling up behind her with the plume of her car's exhaust.

Her first stop was her sister-in-law's shop, Fabrics and Fun. She still needed some backing for the quilt she had made for her newest grandchild. The thought of little Will made her smile. At least Kevin couldn't threaten that, she thought, as she turned onto the road.

Half an hour later she was fingering various bolts of cloth, trying to decide which one to use for the quilt.

"Pretty quiet in here this morning," Charlotte said, glancing around the shop. The material lining the wall and set out on the display racks softened any noise in the shop, creating an aura of peace.

"You just missed a busy run," Rosemary said, re-rolling a bolt of cloth on the cutting table. "I had five ladies from the quilters' guild in here, planning their latest projects. It was like being inside a henhouse at laying time."

Charlotte had to laugh at the analogy.

"But otherwise, it's quiet, like you said. I guess people are staying home, using up the material they already have instead of coming to get more." Rosemary glanced up at Charlotte, her glasses glinting, the gray strands of her hair highlighted by the overhead lights.

Charlotte felt a nudge of melancholy at the sight, knowing her own hair showed more and more gray each time she looked into a mirror. And the events of the past few days were enough to hasten the process.

"Tell me about the children. I heard Kevin was back. That was quite a shock."

"For all of us," Charlotte said. "But we'll just have to deal with it one day at a time."

"You sound so stoic," Rosemary said, looking surprised. "I know I've always been worried that Kevin would come back and cause trouble. Is he? Causing trouble, I mean?"

Charlotte looked away from Rosemary, trying to formulate her thoughts.

Though she had never had children of her own, Rosemary had lived vicariously through Charlotte and Bob. She had celebrated each small victory of their children, the first time their elder son, Bill, slept through the night, the first teeth of each child, the first steps, the first days of school. Rosemary was the one Charlotte had come to when she needed to share her first frustrations about living on the farm and then with having children who didn't always get along.

Charlotte often shared her troubles with Hannah, but she actually thought of Rosemary as the sister she'd never had. She was someone who listened and always offered support.

When Denise died and the children came to stay with Bob and Charlotte almost two years ago, Rosemary had been a huge help. But now she realized Rosemary was getting older herself. And Charlotte didn't think it fair to put all her burdens on her sister-in-law's shoulders.

Besides, she was going to talk to Melody. She would understand.

"He's not causing trouble," Charlotte assured her. "In fact, he's taken them out for dinner and taken them shopping." She fought down a beat of resentment when she thought of the gifts he'd bought the children. She wasn't sure of the exact price of the things he had given them, but she did think it was far too much. "The children are a bit confused, but I'm glad that Kevin is at least showing some concern for them now. I'm glad he's decided to be involved in their lives." As she spoke the upbeat and positive words, Charlotte wished, to the bottom of her heart, that she could be as sincere as she sounded.

"There will be adjustments, I'm sure, but it's all for the good." Rosemary held her gaze, and in her eyes, Charlotte caught a hint of disbelief in her own encouraging words.

Charlotte squeezed Rosemary's hand, thankful for the support. "It will all turn out just fine, Rosemary. I'm not worried." She added a bright smile, hoping Rosemary believed her.

"Well, that's good then," Rosemary said. "Good that you went and visited that lawyer and got everything straightened out."

Charlotte didn't have the heart to tell her that nothing had come of that. "Yes. It's a good thing I did that," she simply said.

Rosemary patted Charlotte on the shoulder and slipped off her stool. "I have to do a few things, but you just sit there and tell me all about your newest grandson. I'm sure Anna and Bill are thrilled, having a boy after two girls."

"He is adorable. I'm looking forward to seeing him on Saturday. Anna's mother gave the go-ahead."

Rosemary tut-tutted as she resumed re-rolling the bolts of cloth on the cutting table. "I've only met her on a few occasions, but I have gotten the impression that she can be a force to be reckoned with. Pete called her Hurricane Helen."

Charlotte stifled a smile. Trust Pete to come up with something like that. "At any rate, this gives me some time to get Will's quilt done before we see them again."

Their talk veered to safer topics concerning the children. From there they moved to the church community and the upcoming Christmas pageant.

"Are the children involved in it this year?" Rosemary was asking.

"Not at all, and frankly, I'm quite relieved. What with Christopher's solo and the whole kerfuffle surrounding Emily taking Nicole's place as Mary last year, I'm quite glad to be away from all the drama."

"And this Christmas, you've got enough going on." Rosemary gave her a quick smile.

And they were back to Kevin.

"Now, let's find you the material you need to finish that quilt. That's what you came here for, right?" Rosemary said, as if only too happy herself to change the subject.

The next few minutes were taken up choosing fabric, and while she looked around, Charlotte found a few more fat quarters to add to her stash.

While Rosemary rang up the purchases, another two women came into the shop.

"I'll give you a call later on. See how things are going." Rosemary handed Charlotte her bag. "And I'll be praying for you."

"Thanks," Charlotte said, lowering her voice. "I appreciate that."

"Sharing quilting secrets?" one of the ladies asked with a too avid look. Like a magpie seeking out treasure, Charlotte thought.

"Is there any other kind?" Charlotte said, forcing a teasing tone into her voice.

The lady frowned at her and then at Rosemary. Obviously this was not the answer she had expected.

Charlotte waved to her sister-in-law and left her to the curious gazes of the two women.

A sharp winter wind swirled down Main Street as Charlotte dropped her bags in the car and crossed over to Mel's Place.

The restaurant was quiet when the frosted glass door fell shut behind her. Charlotte took a moment to savor the welcoming scent of muffins baking, overlaid with the rich scent of coffee.

"Hey, there you are," Melody said from behind the counter. Her hair was wrapped in a printed bandanna that matched her apron. "Find a spot and sit down. Be with you in a flash. I just have to help Ginny get the soup going."

Melody disappeared, and Charlotte chose a table closer to the back, where they would be a bit secluded.

She slipped off her coat and relaxed as the warmth of the café enveloped her.

Two young women sat in one corner, but they were in deep discussion and hadn't seen her come in.

Charlotte toyed with the fake holly centerpiece on the table, letting the Christmas music drifting out of the speakers above the counter soothe her. And as the comfortable environment surrounded her, Charlotte felt herself calm down. She was looking forward to being able to talk about some of the real concerns she had with Kevin that she hadn't been able to discuss with Rosemary.

A minute later, Melody set a couple of steaming mugs of coffee on the table and dropped into the chair across from

Charlotte. "Here you go," she said, pushing a mug toward Charlotte and blowing out her breath in a sigh. "I wanted to talk to you at church, but I must have missed you."

"We had to leave right away because we had to go to see Anna. She had her baby on Saturday."

"How exciting!" Melody squealed. "What did she have?"

"A little boy. Seven pounds, six ounces. His name is Will, after his father and grandfather." Charlotte couldn't help but smile as she recited the information. It seemed more real each time she said it.

"Another grandson. Congratulations," Melody said, nodding her approval. "I'm so glad for you. Do you still have the girls?"

"They went to Anna's mother on Sunday evening." Charlotte picked up the warm mug of coffee, wrapping her chilled hands around it. "So now life is back to normal."

"That's good." Melody dropped a generous spoonful of sugar in her own coffee and gave Charlotte a tight smile. "I wouldn't mind a bit of normal around my house. Ashley has been acting so weird lately, and I'm convinced it has to do with her boyfriend."

"That's Ryan Holt, isn't it?"

Melody nodded. "I like the kid, but the way Ashley's been swooning around the house is getting on my last nerve. She puts on enough makeup to earn our local Mary Kay rep her pink Cadillac. She spends hours and hours getting every single hair on her head just so." Melody lifted her hands in a gesture of surrender and dropped them onto the table. "I'm getting tired of it, but I don't know what to do with the girl. Has Emily said anything about it to you?"

Charlotte shook her head. "She did say something about

it the other night, but when I said she could talk to me if she wanted, she just gave me a vague smile. She's got a lot on her mind as well these days."

Melody released a heavy sigh. "I'm worried about Ashley. Really worried. I'm scared she thinks she's going to lose the boy and she'll end up doing something truly stupid just to try to keep him. She's so over-the-moon crazy about him, it isn't healthy."

"Ashley's a smart girl," Charlotte said, reaching across the table to grasp Melody's hand in hers. "I've always thought she was a steadying influence in Emily's life. I'm sure she'll figure this out as well."

"She better. Soon. Or I'm going to have to sit down and do the mother-daughter talk again." Melody shook her head. "I hate doing that even more than she hates hearing it. But I have to do some kind of intervention. She's not my Ashley anymore. Do you think Emily could talk to her? Say something to her?"

Charlotte felt a disloyal nudge of dismay. She had so hoped, for Emily's sake, that Ashley would be a support for her granddaughter. But it seemed that Ashley had her own problems and now, so did her mother.

For a moment Charlotte felt all alone.

"I'll ask Emily," Charlotte said.

Melody gave her a quick smile of thanks. "I appreciate that." The bells above the door jangled, and Melody turned around to make sure the new customers were being taken care of.

Right behind them came another couple. Looked like the noon rush was starting early.

Melody turned back to Charlotte. "And how are things at the farm?"

"Good. Pete and Dana are making plans, trying to decide what to do about living arrangements."

"That's right," Melody said. "Since that fire on the farm, they can hardly stay in Pete's apartment."

"No, they can't. They've already torn down the old structure and are working on replacing the tractor shed, at least." Charlotte felt her mind go suddenly blank. She couldn't think of any other chitchat to share with her friend.

Melody sat on the edge of her chair, as if ready to take off at any minute.

"If you need to leave, just go ahead," Charlotte said, sensing her restlessness.

Melody frowned at Charlotte and eased back in her chair. "Sorry. I didn't mean to look so antsy. It's just that Ginny has been extra absentminded lately. Friday she put way too much salt in the soup because on Thursday she didn't put in enough." Melody sighed as she leaned her elbows on the table and held Charlotte's gaze.

"You look troubled, my friend," she said. "Something bothering you?"

Charlotte had to smile at her friend's perception. But she realized Melody had enough on her mind now; she didn't need to be burdened with Charlotte's worries too. She waved off Melody's concern. "Just this and that. Christopher and Sam had a fight about Christopher using his college application forms to draw up some plans for Pete and Dana's house, and since then Christopher has been holed up in his bedroom."

Melody smiled. "Sounds like the usual back and forth with kids."

"Yeah. The usual." Charlotte gave her a careful smile. "If you need to get back to work, I'm just waiting for Bob."

Melody frowned. "There's something you're not telling me."

Charlotte gave a quick laugh. "You've got enough happening in your life."

"Don't we all?" Melody leaned forward. "Ashley is just going through a phase. I shouldn't have been so melodramatic about it." Melody touched Charlotte's arm. "I can see by the look on your face that you've got some serious trouble going on. And I'm a friend. So please, let me be a friend. If we have to wait until our own lives are perfectly smooth, we'd never tell each other anything."

Charlotte drew in a breath, as if to draw strength, and sat back. "Kevin is back. He came to the farm."

"Ah, I heard a rumor the other day that someone had seen him, but I didn't believe it." Melody shook her head. "What does he think he's doing? Did you have any idea he was coming?"

"None whatsoever. He just showed up on Saturday. Drove up the driveway and said he wanted to take the kids out for dinner and shopping."

Melody slowly shook her head. "I can't believe this."

"I didn't know what to think either."

"Did he give any reason for staying away so long? For not getting in touch with the kids earlier? For not coming to Denise's funeral?"

"He says he just found out about Denise's death a little

while ago. Then he figured that the kids would have ended up at our place. So he came."

"That's his only reason for coming back?" Melody pressed.

Charlotte hesitated, wondering if it was right to give out too much information.

But she needed to talk to someone. To get some advice. "He says he wants the kids." Her words spilled out.

"That . . . *snake*." Melody fell back against her chair, still shaking her head in disbelief. "How in the world does he think he can just waltz back into the kids' lives and throw this at them?"

"The children don't know anything about that yet," Charlotte said, leaning forward. "So please, please, don't tell anyone."

"No. Of course not. But what are you going to do?"

"Right now? I don't know."

"You have to fight this. You talked to that lawyer in Harding a while back—when you thought Kevin was coming back for his class reunion. Why don't you hire him? Get him to fight for you?"

"I called his office, but he's gone for a while, and I'll have to wait until he gets back." Charlotte thought of the bill the lawyer had sent them after her last visit to him. It had been high enough. She couldn't imagine what a prolonged battle would cost.

The farm had enough financial obligations without having to take on legal bills to fight Kevin. And they had the children's futures to think about.

As well, did she and Bob have the fortitude to endure a drawn-out battle with Kevin?

"Bob and I need to talk to him, that's for sure," Charlotte said, picking up her mug and taking another sip.

For the merest moment she understood what Bob had been complaining about only a few days ago. Taking the children on, at times, seemed to be more than they could handle.

But as quickly as the thought came she banished it. She loved her grandchildren and would do anything for them. Including taking on Kevin if she and Bob had to.

"How are you feeling about all this?" Melody asked.

Charlotte put her coffee down, her emotions washing over her like a wave. She had been wanting to talk to someone besides Bob ever since Kevin had burst into their lives.

"It's been like a roller coaster..." Her words faded away as she tried to find a way to let her friend know exactly what it had been like for her. The frustration. The worry. The concern.

Then a movement behind Melody caught her eye. Someone was walking toward their table.

It was Kevin himself.

Chapter Fourteen

"Hello, Charlotte. Fancy meeting you here." Kevin stood beside them, the dusting of snow on his leather jacket melting in the heat of the restaurant. His hair was damp and his cheeks red from the chill. He gave Charlotte a tight smile and then glanced over at Melody.

"Melody, you remember Kevin Slater," Charlotte said.

"And I remember you, Melody," Kevin said, shaking Melody's hand, his brow puckered in a thoughtful frown. "You were friends with Denise, right?"

Melody looked up at him, her eyes narrowing. "I was sorry to hear about her death. And very sad. We were close at one time."

Kevin nodded, looking solemn. "Thank you. It's still kind of hard to believe that she's gone."

Charlotte did not honestly know whether he was simply mouthing platitudes or if he sincerely meant what he was saying. His previous actions certainly didn't show the remorse he seemed to be showing now.

"She was a good friend," Melody said.

In the moment of silence following Mel's statement, Charlotte felt once again the pain of her own loss. Even though it had been more than a year and a half since that horrible phone call shattered her life and Bob's, there were times the sorrow snuck up on her, unaware.

And seeing Kevin again seemed to underscore the pain.

"So what brings you back to Bedford?" Melody asked, looking up at Kevin.

Kevin smiled. "Well, my kids of course."

"*Your* kids?" Melody's incredulous tone seemed to cut through the air.

Kevin pulled back. "Yeah. My kids."

Melody raised her eyebrows and Charlotte sensed a confrontation coming on. Melody wasn't one to mince words, and she had made her own feelings about Kevin fairly clear from time to time.

Though Charlotte tended to agree with her assessment of Kevin's behavior, she didn't want to antagonize him.

"Kevin, what have you been keeping busy with?" Charlotte asked, intervening before Melody gave him the piece of her mind she had always threatened she would share if she ever ran into him again.

Kevin grabbed a chair and straddled it, his smile slipping so easily back in place it made Charlotte uncomfortable.

"I just went wandering around town. Checked out some of the places Denise and I used to go to. Went by the school."

Charlotte nodded. "That's where the kids are now."

The door chimes rang out again, and Melody glanced over her shoulder.

"That Ginny," she muttered. "Still hasn't helped all the customers."

Melody shot Charlotte an apologetic look. "Sorry. I gotta take care of business."

"Of course. You go ahead," Charlotte said, though she was very sorry to see Melody leave. Right now she could use the moral support.

As Melody left, Kevin turned back to Charlotte. "I, uh, figured on picking the kids up from school today. Maybe take them out again."

Charlotte suffered a moment of confusion but knew she had to hold her ground. "I don't think that's a good idea."

"Why not?"

"Well . . . for one thing, you didn't tell me or Bob."

"They're my kids. I wouldn't think I have to run everything by you." Kevin's tone took on an angry edge that increased Charlotte's discomfort.

"I think telling me your plans would be best," Charlotte said. "Your return into their lives is new and strange for them. They still don't know you that well."

"I'm their father. And the only way they'll get to know me is if I spend time with them."

"I realize that," Charlotte said, trying to placate him. "But at the same time, they have their own lives and their own responsibilities here, and they need routine."

Goodness knows it had been hard enough to get the kids settled into a routine when they moved to the farm. At times, Charlotte felt like she still struggled to find a new normal to their lives.

"I have my rights, you know," Kevin shot back, rocking back and forth on the chair.

Please, Lord, don't let me get angry, Charlotte prayed,

struggling to find the right way to say what needed to be said.

"I'm sure you do. But right now, the most important thing we have to be concerned about is the children and what they need." She sat back, folding her arms across her chest.

"They need their dad," Kevin blustered. "They've already lost their mother."

"They've needed their dad for a whole lot longer than the past few days."

The words spilled out before she could stop them, and from the way Kevin's face darkened, Charlotte knew she had just made an enemy out of their son-in-law.

Kevin swung his leg over the chair and stood, gripping the back of it. "You think I'm a lousy father, don't you?"

Charlotte took a moment to gather her thoughts, to find exactly the right thing to say.

"I think it's important that the children have you in their lives," she replied, trying to hold his gaze. "But I also think it's important that they maintain their routine."

Kevin snorted at that, his eyes darting around, looking anywhere but at her. "I remember Denise talking about your precious *routine*." He made quotation marks with his fingers around the last word. "She hated it. Said that was why she ran away. With me. And I don't think I want my kids living like that." This time he did look at her, and Charlotte fought to keep the pain his words had inflicted from showing.

"But just to keep the peace," Kevin continued, "I'll leave them alone today and figure on picking them up on Saturday at five."

Charlotte simply nodded, not trusting herself to speak as her heart pounded with a mixture of fear and sorrow.

He held her gaze a moment, as if to challenge her. She forced herself not to look away.

Then, at last, Kevin left.

Charlotte's breath left her, like air out of a stale balloon. She pressed her fingers to her temples, massaging away the tension that had gripped her since Kevin walked into the restaurant.

Could she and Bob see this through to the end?

And what would be the end? Kevin out of the children's lives?

Kevin showing up, testing and pushing the boundaries they had set in place?

The children out of their lives?

That she couldn't bear.

Please, Lord, she prayed, *help us find the wisdom to deal with Kevin. Help us show him that the children need to stay with us. That they need to be on the farm. I can't lose them, Lord. I simply can't.*

She took another breath as her heart slowly settled. She had to get in touch with Marcus Lindstrom, their lawyer in Harding. She had to get things settled as quickly as she could. She should have done that the first time they thought Kevin was coming back into the children's lives, but she had let sentimentality override her common sense. She wasn't going to let that happen again. She hoped he would be available to help them soon.

"Charlotte, are you okay?" Bob's voice broke into her scrambled thoughts.

Charlotte jumped, then gave Bob a quick smile. "Yes. I'm fine."

"That's good," he said, slipping into the chair across from her. He glanced down at Melody's coffee cup. "Who was sitting here?"

"Melody. But she's busy with her customers," Charlotte said. She took another breath. "Did you see Kevin?"

Bob frowned. "No. Was he here?"

Charlotte nodded. "He just left. He said he was picking up the children after school."

"He can't do that. Not without running it by us first."

Relief seeped through her. She wasn't being controlling. Bob agreed with her. "That's what I told him."

Bob pushed the coffee cup aside, leaning his elbows on the table. "We need to lay down some ground rules. He may think he's getting the kids, but we still need to set out when and where he can see them in the meantime."

"I agree." She was about to say more when Melody bustled up to the table and pulled forward the same chair Kevin had just vacated.

"That Kevin's a piece of work." She shook her head. "Sorry I had to bail on you, but Ginny was being an airhead again." Melody glanced from Bob to Charlotte. "I was telling Charlotte you should hire that lawyer again. Get him to fight for you."

Bob nodded briefly. "That's a possibility."

"You can't let Kevin get away with this," Melody said. "You have to fight fire with fire. Come at him with what you've got—and you've got a lot. He hasn't seen the kids since he left Denise. He never sent her money. If it goes to court, no judge on earth would award him custody over you."

"We have a few decisions to make," Bob said, his tone cryptic.

Charlotte gave her friend's arm a gentle squeeze of warning. In some ways, her husband could be very old-fashioned, and receiving vociferous advice from a woman closer to his daughter's age than his might not sit well with him.

Melody seemed to take the hint, but Charlotte could see from the way she pinched her lips that she wasn't finished yet.

"Well, if there's anything Russ or I can do, let us know," Melody said. "We'd like to help."

"Thanks, Melody. I really appreciate the support."

They gave their orders and when she left, Bob and Charlotte were alone again.

"I'm going to call the lawyer again," Charlotte said.

"His office said he isn't going to be back for awhile yet, so I doubt he's going to return your call. We'll have to see how hard Kevin pushes before we decide what we're doing."

Panic clawed at Charlotte. "He told us very clearly what he wants. He said he was going to fight us for the children."

Bob scratched the side of his face with a forefinger as he thought. His cuticles were edged with grease from the work he had been doing on the tractor. It seemed there was always something to fix, something that needed money spent on it.

The thought of going to a lawyer, of spending more money just to stake their claim on the children, bothered her on one level. Yet they couldn't afford to simply stand aside and let Kevin do what he wanted without fighting back as, it seemed, Bob was suggesting.

"Kevin hasn't always followed through on what he has said he would do," Bob said, his voice growing quiet.

Charlotte knew, on one level, that Bob was right, but to simply sit back and wait ... she didn't know if she could do that. Her mothering instinct was to fight tooth and nail for her grandchildren.

Then Melody appeared with their order and the conversation ended. It seemed nothing more needed to be said, but Charlotte didn't enjoy her food at all. A few minutes later she pushed it away and wiped her mouth. "I better get back home," she said. "I need to bake bread and get the laundry done. And I want to get ready for Saturday."

"What's Saturday?" Bob asked.

"Bill, Anna, and the children are coming over. I wanted to have a little lunch party to welcome Will to the family."

"Why don't you have a dinner?"

"Because Kevin is coming at five to take the kids out again; that's why."

Bob simply nodded, still eating his sandwich.

Charlotte slipped her purse over her shoulder. "Are you coming home soon?"

"I was going to stop and see the guys at the fire hall. But I'll be home after that."

Charlotte nodded, wishing, for once, that she could as easily keep the various parts of her life separate as Bob seemed to.

The afternoon slipped by, and the routine of her work brought Charlotte some peace of mind. The yeasty scent of bread baking, the warmth of the stove steaming up the windows, creating a haze between the cozy kitchen and the cold outside, soothed her worries away.

The door of the porch banged open, and chilly winter air crept across the floor.

"Are the kids home?" Pete asked loudly. His words were accompanied by the rustling of plastic bags.

"Not yet." Curious, Charlotte walked to the porch in time to meet Pete coming into the kitchen, his arms laden with bags.

"What's this?"

Pete's cheeks were red, his eyes bright. He set the parcels on the kitchen table, their contents spilling out. "Christmas presents for the kids. I want you to let me know what you think."

Charlotte frowned. "But we drew names this year, Pete. And we promised we were buying only for the person whose name we drew."

Pete waved away Charlotte's protests. "I know, but I wanted to get the kids something special from their Uncle Pete." He opened one bag and pulled out a box. "These are for Emily. I don't know if they're the right size, but she can exchange them if she doesn't like them." He pulled a pair of knee-length leather boots out of the box. "The lady at the store in Harding told me this is exactly what girls like Emily go for these days." He flashed Charlotte a cheeky grin. "Told her that she dresses kind of strange."

He grabbed another bag and pulled out a gray-and-green hooded sweatshirt. "This is for Sam, and I got a matching one for Christopher. Thought that would be kinda neat. I also got a bunch of DVDs ..." He pawed through the bags, looking, as Charlotte put her hand on his arm, stopping him mid-search.

"Pete, what are you trying to do?"

Pete reared back. "I'm trying to be an uncle. Trying to have some fun with my nephews and niece. That's all."

He sounded all blustery and defensive, and though Charlotte appreciated the generosity, she wasn't so sure of the motives. She was careful as she formulated her words. "This isn't about the expensive things that Kevin bought the children the other day?"

Pete shook his head, his hand slicing through the air as if cutting that idea off. "No way. No how. I just thought it was time I did something for the kids. And I don't think there's anything wrong with me giving them a few things from time to time. Don't do it often enough, I think."

"And what about Jennifer, Madison, and Will? Did you think it was time to do something for them?"

That stopped Pete mid-bluster. His blush grew, and he glanced away. "Well, I could get them something tomorrow."

Charlotte sighed and placed her hand on Pete's arm. "Pete, I think it's wonderful that you want to give gifts to the kids, but I don't think you should be buying them such expensive things."

"You don't think I can afford it?"

Charlotte paused, praying for wisdom.

"I don't think you *should* afford it. Right now your first priority is Dana and the life you are planning to make with her."

Pete slumped into a chair, pushing aside a bag on the table. He sighed. "And that's the trouble," he said, dismay edging his voice. "I feel like I don't even know what kind of life I can plan for Dana and me. That Kevin dude is throwing money around like there's no end in sight, and I know he's buying the kids stuff they like. And on top of all of that, I feel like I can't even provide a home for my future wife. It's not a good feeling, Mom."

Charlotte sat down across from him, resisting the urge to stroke his head like she used to when he was younger and his problems were so much easier to solve.

"It wasn't your fault that we had that fire. You were making a lovely place for Dana, and something happened. Now you have to adapt to the change in plans." Charlotte hoped he would understand. All his life Pete had struggled with feelings of inadequacy. He often felt less successful than his older brother, and now that Pete was getting married, she guessed he was once again comparing his situation to Bill's.

And now, on top of all that, he was trying to compete with Kevin as well.

Pete slouched back into his chair, his hand brushing one of the bags on the table. He pulled it toward him and took out a large plastic container holding a cell-phone case covered in bright yellow daisies. "This was for Emily," he said quietly. "For her cell phone." He dropped it on the table with a sigh. "I was mad. That's why I bought this stuff."

"Mad at Kevin?" Charlotte prompted.

Pete shook his head. "Mad at myself. Here's this guy only a few years older than me and he's got a fancy truck, a great job, he travels, and he makes enough money that he can buy the kids whatever he wants."

"His money can only buy *things*," Charlotte said.

"And any minute now you're going to tell me that money can't buy love," Pete said, flipping the container over and over in his hands.

"It can't, Pete. Kevin is not a happy person, and he only has his money. He doesn't seem to have much else. He doesn't have family, and he certainly doesn't have someone like Dana."

"Bet if he did, he could buy her a house."

"He had someone like Dana. Your sister. And look what he did to her. They lived in an apartment their entire married life, and then he left her alone with three children." Charlotte's anger with Kevin spilled out into her voice. "So don't you even begin to start comparing yourself to that man. You are ten times the man he is, and I'm very proud of what you've done with your life. You've been responsible. You've helped us out in so many ways, and now you're going to marry a wonderful woman and start your own life together. You can hold your head up high for who you are and what you've accomplished."

She stopped, surprised herself at how vehement she had been, how emotional. That wasn't like her.

But her son was putting himself down, and that wasn't right.

Pete gave her a funny look. "You really mean that, don't you?"

"I wouldn't say it if I didn't. And I know your father, even though he might not tell you in so many words, feels the same way." Charlotte knew that Pete and his father shared an awkward affection for each other. But she also knew they seldom let each other know.

As Pete put the plastic container back in the bag, he said, "I guess the short answer is, I shouldn't give these to the kids?"

Charlotte shook her head. "Please don't. Their father is already spending far too much on them. They don't need any more presents."

Pete sighed and looked over at the bags. "So what should I do with this stuff?"

"If you have the receipts, you could take them back."

Pete snorted. "That's embarrassing."

"Well, maybe, but I think it's hard to justify this expense when you and Dana are planning a wedding."

"I suppose." He shook his head as if trying to understand where his priorities should be.

"Getting them all these things was a wonderful idea in its own way, Pete," Charlotte said, covering his hand, trying to assure him. "And you showed amazing ingenuity. But it isn't necessary. In ten years the kids will have better memories about the rides you gave them on the snowmobile than they will about the presents their dad or even you bought for them."

A reluctant smile crept across Pete's face, and Charlotte sensed that he finally believed what she was telling him and was taking it to heart.

"I don't suppose you'd be willing to return this stuff for me?" Pete said, picking up one of the bags.

Charlotte shook her head. "I don't have time." Then she held her hand up. "But wait a minute. I have Christopher's name. I have absolutely no idea what to get him. What did you get for him? Maybe I can pay you back for it?"

So they went through the gifts and Charlotte chose the hoodie that was supposed to match Sam's. That meant one less item Pete would have to return, and one more thing off Charlotte's to-do list.

Pete put the rest of the items back in the bags and then sighed. "It seemed like such a good idea at the time, but you're probably right."

Charlotte put her hand on Pete's shoulder. "You need to save your money for your wedding and your future with Dana. And the children certainly don't need more presents that can get in the way of the real meaning of Christmas."

Pete chuckled. "Once again you've proven that Mom knows best."

"Sometimes," she said with a laugh. "Only sometimes."

Chapter Fifteen

Emily pulled the box holding her camera onto her lap and sighed. Having this amazing camera was supposed to be fun, but she still felt funny about getting it from her father. She wished Ashley were here to talk to.

She picked up her cell phone and then put it down again, remembering how Ashley was the last time they saw each other.

Her friend was probably too busy to call her. Too busy with Ryan and his sister. Too busy trying to figure out how to do her hair to impress him.

Emily shook her head. Other people would think she was jealous of the fact that Ashley had a boyfriend and she didn't. And maybe, in one tiny way, she was.

But mostly she just wished she had her friend back again.

She heard the house phone ring, but this time she didn't jump up to try to get it from Uncle Pete's room. Probably wasn't for her anyway. Ashley usually called her on her cell.

Besides, the last few times the phone had rung, the ringing had come from Christopher's room, which was unusual. Christopher hardly ever used the phone.

Maybe he'd been phoning his friend Dylan.

Emily rested her chin in her hands, looking at the camera box and deciding it might be fun to take it out and start experimenting with it.

"Emily, phone's for you," Charlotte called up the stairs.

Emily's heart jumped. Ashley?

"I'll get it upstairs." Emily ran into Uncle Pete's room, but the extension wasn't on the cradle. She didn't feel like digging through Christopher's room to get it so she went downstairs to take the call.

She took the handset from her grandmother, wondering who was calling her. "Hello?"

"Hey, Emily."

Emily's heart fell. "Hey, Megan. How are you?"

"I'm okay. Hey, have you talked to Ashley lately?"

"Not recently," Emily said, trying not to let her frustration with her friend slip into her voice. "Why?"

"She has my pink cardigan, and I'd like to get it back, but she's not talking to me either."

"Ashley's kind of busy with her boyfriend," Emily said. "I wouldn't count on seeing your sweater anytime soon."

"I suppose. I thought maybe you could ask her about it. Seeing as you're her best friend."

"Used to be," Emily snapped and then wished she hadn't said anything. Megan didn't need to know that. "But next time I see her, I'll ask, okay?"

"That would be great. Thanks."

Emily pressed the button to end the call and looked at the phone a minute, feeling an inexplicable urge to call Ashley.

"Friend troubles?" Grandma asked, looking up from the cookbook she had out on the kitchen table. The dishwasher swished through its cycle, and from the family room some guy yelled from the television set to come and buy a new vehicle—now.

Grandpa, snoring on his recliner, was oblivious, as was Uncle Pete, stretched out on the couch, reading some farm magazine. Sam lay on the floor, playing a game on Christopher's Nintendo. Christopher was up in his room, probably still sulking about Sam getting angry with him for writing on his applications.

Life in the Stevenson household on a Friday evening, Emily thought, wondering, for a split second, what her dad was doing. Was he sitting in a motel room all by himself?

She pushed that thought aside as she turned back to her grandmother.

"Megan just wanted to know if Ashley had her sweater."

Grandma frowned. "Why was she asking you?"

"She hasn't been able to talk to Ashley either."

Emily couldn't help sounding ticked off about Ashley. She had all this stuff roiling around in her head, and she didn't know what to think about it. What was the point of having a friend if you couldn't talk to her about the big stuff on your mind?

Just for a moment Emily wanted to drop into the kitchen chair and spill everything to Grandma that she wanted to talk to Ashley about. How, in one way, she was glad her dad was back, and how one small part of her wondered what it would be like to live with him. And how she was also annoyed at him for showing up out of the blue.

She remembered how, when she was little and things were tough, when they were living with her mom, she would daydream about her dad. Pretend that he would come swooping into their lives to rescue them and buy them all the things they wanted but couldn't afford.

Now he had shown up, and he had bought them stuff with the promise of more to come. Though part of her liked that, part of her did not.

"I hope you and Ashley can make up," Grandma said, giving Emily a careful smile. "I was talking to Melody yesterday when I was in town. She's worried about Ashley too. She said Ashley isn't acting like herself."

Emily thought about Ashley's nail polish, the new hairstyle, and the extra makeup, and she nodded in agreement. "It's like she's a whole other person. Especially when she's around Ryan's sister. Then she gets really weird."

"You sound angry about that. I hope you and Ashley aren't in a fight."

"No. We're not in a fight. You have to actually be talking to each other to be in a fight."

"You're not talking?"

"Not lately."

"Would it maybe be a good idea to make the first move?"

Emily tossed the handset of the phone back and forth, thinking of all the first moves she had made. She had sent texts, had tried to talk to Ashley, had made a fool of herself in the cafeteria.

"I've wanted to ever since my dad came back." Emily stopped there, sneaking a quick peek at her grandmother to get her reaction to that. But Grandma just looked at her like she didn't even notice. Emily continued, "But on Sunday she practically ignored me, and she hasn't been answering my text messages. And when I saw her in the cafeteria Monday she was acting all flirty and silly around Ryan. I don't know what's going on with her."

Grandma didn't say anything for a minute, and Emily thought maybe she wasn't that interested.

"Do you think Ashley might be worried about her boyfriend?"

"Ryan? What's to worry about? He seems pretty crazy about her . . ." But even as Emily spoke the words, her mind ticked back to the way Ryan had been acting around Ashley. Like he wasn't paying much attention to her.

"I know Melody seemed concerned about Ashley and Ryan's relationship." Grandma touched Emily on the arm. "I know you've had a lot on your mind lately, but Melody asked if you wouldn't mind talking to Ashley."

Emily looked down at the phone she still held. "But she's always too busy to talk to me."

"Still, she's your friend. Melody thinks Ashley might confide in you. Maybe you could give her some advice?"

Emily laughed at that. "Me? Advice? Ashley is the one who always has her act together. Ashley is the one who's always telling *me* how to behave."

Grandma gave her a smile that seemed a bit melancholy.

"Sometimes what you *see* isn't what's really there. Sometimes what's on the surface can be hiding what's below. You have more strength than you might realize."

Emily got the feeling Grandma was talking about more than Ashley, but she didn't want to examine that too closely right now. "Do you think Ashley might be hiding something?"

"Maybe you should ask her. As a friend. Be straightforward with her. Don't give up on her. Friends should be there for each other always."

Emily couldn't help but think of her own mother. Once upon a time her mom and Ashley's mom were friends too. But when her mom ran away with their dad, she hadn't told Ashley's mom what she was planning to do.

She didn't want the same thing to happen between her and Ashley. Emily wrinkled her nose and then got up, still holding the phone. "I suppose I could try."

As she walked up the stairs, she punched in Ashley's number, still wondering what she was going to say to her, and then realizing Ashley probably wasn't even home.

It was Friday night. Date night for those who had boyfriends and, well, dates.

To her surprise, however, Ashley answered on the first ring. "Ryan?" she said, sounding breathless.

"Sorry. It's just me," Emily replied, dropping onto her bed.

"Oh. Hey."

Well, let's not get too excited now.

"Hey yourself. What's up?" Emily picked at a piece of lint on her pants, not sure where to go from here.

"Nothing. Nothing much."

Emily frowned, her ears pricking up. Was Ashley crying? "Are you okay?" she asked.

"Yeah. Why wouldn't I be?"

Emily hesitated. Ashley sounded mad. But then she heard another sniff, and she knew something was really wrong with her friend. "You don't sound okay. What's wrong?"

Ashley didn't reply right away, but Emily didn't say anything. Just waited.

"Everything's wrong," Ashley cried. "Everything."

"What do you mean? Is it Ryan?"

"Yeah. He's hardly paying any attention to me anymore. It's like he doesn't even know I exist."

Emily thought back to that moment in the cafeteria and to what her grandmother said.

"I've tried to do everything his sister told me to do, but it's not helping," Ashley continued.

"Wait a minute. What do you mean, everything his sister told you to do? Why are you taking advice from her?" Emily didn't know Ryan's sister real well, but she knew enough that she didn't care for her. It had bothered her when she saw that Ashley and Ryan were double-dating with his sister and her boyfriend.

Ashley sighed. "Well, it all started a couple of weeks ago when Ryan was supposed to call me back, and then he said he forgot. I said something to him about it in front of his sister, Malinda, and she pulled me aside and started giving me all kinds of advice on how to keep Ryan. She said he was losing interest and that we should go on double dates..." Ashley broke off then, and Emily heard another sniff.

"Is that why you started wearing all the makeup?" Emily asked as an idea slowly started to formulate.

"Yeah. Ryan was acting a bit weird, and I needed some advice on how to keep him."

And suddenly her friend's behavior made a bit more sense. But in spite of that Emily was still upset with her. "Why didn't you ask *me*?"

"Malinda is Ryan's sister."

"That doesn't mean she knows what's best for you," Emily said. "I thought we were friends. And friends help each other."

Still no answer from Ashley, and Emily wondered if she had said too much. Then she heard a click, as if someone wanted to use the phone. She waited a minute, but then nothing. If it was Grandma she would have said something.

Maybe it was Sam.

Well, she wasn't going to let him use the phone just yet. She had finally connected with her friend, and she had something to say.

"We went through this when you and Ryan started going out," she said. "It hurt then, and it hurts even more now. If you keep wondering if he's going to dump you then maybe he's not the guy for you."

"Why are you being so mean?" Ashley said, her voice breaking just a little.

Emily felt bad, but right now, it seemed to her that her own troubles were a lot bigger than Ashley's. "I needed you, Ashley. I needed to talk to you. I left you all kinds of messages, and you never answered because you were too busy listening to someone who doesn't care about you as much as I do."

"I'm sorry I didn't answer your messages; it was just that I was so busy..."

"With Ryan. I get that. Well, you need to figure out where to put me in your life. I get that you have a boyfriend, but that doesn't mean you leave your friends all alone when they're having problems too." Emily stopped, her own voice breaking. "I'm not trying to make you choose between me and Ryan, but I needed you, and you weren't there."

Emily bit her lip, blinking back the tears that filled her eyes. "I'm sorry. I can't talk anymore right now."

She carefully disconnected the call and then leaned back against her headboard, letting the tears flow down her cheeks, wondering if she had been too mean. If maybe she had lost any chance of making up with Ashley.

For a moment she felt like praying, talking to God like Grandma often suggested she do.

Emily pulled in a trembling sigh and closed her eyes. "Okay, Lord. I don't know what I'm supposed to do. And I'm all mixed up, and I don't want to be. I don't know who else to talk to. Grandma and Grandpa have their own problems, and everyone else is busy. I hope You're not." She waited a minute, as if she should see if she was going to hear anything back. Then she quietly said, "Amen."

She let go another sigh, and though she didn't hear any angels singing or any voice from God, she still felt as if a bit of weight had slipped off her shoulders.

Then she got up to put the phone away.

As she opened the door from her room, she heard Christopher's voice coming from his bedroom. Was he the one who had been trying to use the phone?

Curious, she walked over to his door. She hesitated, feeling like a snoop, but Christopher had been acting kind of funny lately. He'd been spending extra time in his room, and Emily was as worried about him as it seemed Ashley's mom was about her daughter.

"Sam is mad . . . I hate him . . ." was all she could hear from where she stood. Shocked at Christopher's language, she stepped closer, wondering if she should go inside.

"And Emily is kind of pouty lately, and Pete and Miss Simons don't like my house plans . . . from the magazines . . . I know. I had such good ideas for their house . . . I think it stinks too."

Emily frowned. Surely Christopher wasn't talking this angrily to his friend Dylan?

"Sam is playing with my new Nintendo, and I told him that you bought it for me and he said I was a spoiled little boy. But I didn't say that to him about his silly iPod. And he still didn't apologize for getting mad at me for drawing on his papers, and I didn't even do it on purpose. I wish I could stay with you and get away from everyone here."

Emily felt a sudden jolt of awareness. Christopher was talking to their father.

"I'm glad you like to talk to me too," Christopher was saying. "And I miss you too." He paused, and then Emily heard him say, "Maybe I would want to live with you. I think it could be fun too. I don't know if Sam and Emily would . . . I could ask them . . . Okay. I won't say anything."

Emily shivered, as if someone had doused her with ice water. What was Christopher doing? Making plans with their father?

Or, for that matter, what was their father doing?

She didn't know what to do. Walk away and act as if she hadn't heard this conversation? Or barge in and grab the phone away from Christopher and tell her dad to leave them alone?

Because, part of the trouble was, she didn't want their dad to leave them alone, but she didn't know if she wanted to be with him either.

It was so hard.

"I gotta go," Christopher was saying.

Emily pushed herself away from his door and tiptoed back to her bedroom. She waited in the doorway until she heard Christopher's door open. Then she walked through, trying to look casual, as if she had just happened to come out of her room.

Christopher was bringing the handset back to the spare room.

"Oh, hey, Christopher," Emily said. "Who were you phoning?" She said it in a teasing way, like she thought he was calling a girl.

Christopher spun around, his face turning red. "No one."

"Oh, c'mon, you can tell me," she said, making her voice go all singsongy, winking at him as if she was teasing him.

"It wasn't a girl, if that's what you're thinking."

And the Oscar goes to Emily Slater! she thought. "Then who was it?"

"I told you. No one."

Emily pretended to look puzzled. "You said it wasn't a girl."

Christopher looked down, his blush going all the way up to his hairline. "I just...was talking...to a friend."

Emily knew she should quit, but it bothered her that Christopher lied about talking to their dad. "Was it Dylan?"

Christopher shook his head.

"Someone new then?"

Christopher avoided looking at her, obviously uncomfortable.

"Who was it then?" Emily pressed.

"Doesn't matter who it was," Christopher said, raising his voice. "Just leave me alone, Emily."

"Hey, what's going on up here?" Sam came into the hallway, glancing from Emily to Christopher. "Why are you bugging Christopher?"

"I'm not bugging him."

"She is so," Christopher said, sounding really angry now. "She's asking me about who I'm phoning."

Sam glanced down at the phone. "Who were you talking to?"

"I was just talking to my friend and he listens to me and he thinks I'm important and he doesn't treat me like a little kid that everyone just puts up with." Christopher glared at Sam, but when he turned to Emily she saw his lower lip quiver just a bit.

What was he so upset about? Why did he think their dad was such a good friend to him, and why was he hiding the fact that he had talked to him?

"No one cares about me," Christopher said. Then he turned and ran back into his room, taking the phone with him.

Sam frowned at Emily. "What did you do to him?"

"I didn't do anything to him." She glanced at Christopher's door, wondering if she should tell Sam what was going on.

"Is everything okay up there?" Grandma called up the stairs.

"Yeah. It's all good," Emily called back.

"Sam, are you getting those papers you said you needed?"

"Yeah, Grandma. I'll be right down." Sam rolled his eyes.

"What's wrong with you?" Emily asked.

Sam blew out a sigh. "I wish everyone would get off my case about this college stuff. I'm getting sick of it."

"But you have to make a decision, Sam," Emily said.

"No. I don't." Sam shoved his hands in his pockets. "Maybe I should just do what Dad said and go work construction."

"You can't do that," Emily said, horrified that he would even think such a thing. The idea that he wouldn't go to college seemed crazy.

"I can do whatever I want," Sam said. "Besides, if I get a job right out of school, maybe I can afford to buy a decent present for my girlfriend." Sam pushed his hair back from his face and trudged off to his bedroom.

Emily looked from Christopher's room to Sam's. It seemed both boys thought their dad was full of good advice and help.

Nervousness fluttered through her. Too many things were changing too quickly.

She thought of Ashley and wished she hadn't gotten so angry with her. Wished she could call her up and talk to her again.

But she had closed that door by hanging up on her friend. She doubted Ashley would want to talk to her for a while . . . just when she needed her friend more than ever.

Chapter Sixteen

Charlotte glanced around the house. All was in order. From upstairs came the whine of the vacuum cleaner, letting her know that Emily was almost finished with her Saturday chores.

A cake sat on the platter; another plate full of cookies and squares sat beside it. A bright new tablecloth covered the table. Everything was ready for her little party.

Well, not so little anymore. It had started out as simply a family tea. Then Hannah found out, and Charlotte invited her and Frank to come. Then Charlotte felt she should invite Rosemary, and Pete invited Dana, and now it was a full-blown party.

Charlotte felt a genuine flush of excitement. She hadn't seen Will for almost a week, and she was sure he had changed since then.

The sound of a car's engine sent her scurrying to the window. Through the frost-crusted pane she saw Hannah and Frank get out of their truck. Hannah carried a cake tray in her mittened hands. Charlotte should have guessed her old friend wouldn't come empty-handed. As they came up the walk, Rosemary's car pulled up beside their truck. She also took out a container.

Looked like she was going to come out ahead in the baking department, Charlotte thought as she pulled off her apron, ran her hands over her hair, and hurried to the door.

She ushered her guests from the porch where they stamped the snow off their boots into the living room. "Congratulations," Hannah sang out, handing Charlotte the cake tray. She hung her coat up, fluffing up her hair. Then she turned to Charlotte. "What do you think?" she asked, smoothing her hands down the front of her bright red sweatshirt. "I finished embroidering it today."

A green Christmas tree full of lights and ornaments emblazoned the front of the sweatshirt. Charlotte chuckled to herself at her friend's outlandish style.

"It's very Christmasy," was all she could manage.

Hannah would never win any fashion prizes, but her sweatshirt was very festive, to say the least.

Hannah grinned. "Frank says I got a bit carried away, but I was having too much fun, and I wanted to get rid of a bunch of embroidery thread." She pointed at the cake tray Charlotte had set down. "Just some snacks I pulled out of the freezer."

"You didn't have to," Charlotte protested. And truly, she didn't. Charlotte had done more than enough Christmas baking the past few days to keep their family in cookies, squares, and cake until Easter.

"Just put it in the freezer if you don't need it." Hannah turned to Rosemary, who was pulling off her gloves. "So, how's business?"

Rosemary gave her a broad smile. "Just fine. I'm having a sale on embroidery thread, if you're interested."

Hannah flapped her hand at Rosemary. "Now you're teasing me."

While they chatted, Bill and Anna's vehicle pulled into the driveway. The guests of honor were here.

Jennifer and Madison burst up the porch steps and through the front door, filling the room with excited laughter, calling out for Grandma.

Emily and Sam came downstairs, and Bob came out of the family room to greet Hannah, Frank, and Rosemary.

"Grandma, we brought our play clothes," Jennifer sang, tugging at her coat. Underneath she wore an off-white dress edged with bronze-colored lace. A matching bronze ribbon already hung askew in her hair.

Madison had entered the room more primly, dressed in a matching outfit, only her ribbon was straight and her dress didn't have a smudge of brown on the back, as Jennifer's did. She gave her grandmother a sedate hug, walked over to Bob, and did the same. Then she shook Hannah's hand and hugged Rosemary.

The perfect little girl, Charlotte thought, smiling. Anna had trained her well. Jennifer, well, she was another story. If it weren't for the fact that she was a slightly disheveled version of Anna, Charlotte could be forgiven for wondering if Jennifer even belonged to her.

"Can we go tubing afterward?" Jennifer asked, grabbing Emily by the hand and dancing in a circle.

"Maybe," Emily said, humoring her young cousin. "We have to ask your mom and dad."

"They said it's okay." Jennifer pulled Emily toward the porch. "Come and see my baby brother."

Charlotte greeted Bill and Anna and then took the car seat holding her youngest grandchild and gently carried it to the kitchen table. She unzipped the blue plush covering and looked down on the little bundle.

Will's mouth was puckered up, his eyes were scrunched closed, and his head, so tiny, lay askew. He looked lost in the blue velour sleeper he wore, the cuffs rolled up to reveal tiny hands, with their dimpled knuckles, clenched tight.

"You can take him out if you want," Anna said, slipping off her own coat. "He's been sleeping all the way here, though I don't know how. Jennifer was checking on him every couple of minutes."

Charlotte carefully unbuckled Will and eased the straps past his tiny body and nestled him in the crook of her arm. A wave of love, pure and fresh, washed over her. "What a blessing you are," she murmured, brushing the gentlest kiss over his downy forehead.

The porch door flew open once again. "Dana brought more cake," Pete sang out as the noise level in the house increased to a comfortable buzz.

A few minutes later everyone was settled in the living room, some sitting on kitchen chairs, some on the couch as Christmas music played quietly from the stereo. Will, oblivious to the attention lavished on him, got passed around while Anna opened the gifts people had brought. Because she hadn't been feeling well with this pregnancy, she had refused to let anyone throw her a baby shower.

Charlotte looked around the room filled with noise and

laughter as warmth and happiness welled up within her. She was richly blessed. She knew this. And the best way to keep knowing this, she realized, was to accept and appreciate the blessings of each day. She had to be careful not to look too far into the future, wondering what was coming next.

"How are the wedding plans coming along?" Anna was asking Dana.

Dana peered up from a wedding magazine she was looking at with Emily. "We're doing okay," she said. "A little behind schedule, what with the fire and trying to figure out where Pete and I are going to live."

"But surely you have the ceremony planned."

"Some parts of it, yes," Dana said carefully.

"If you haven't chosen music for the ceremony, I know of a wonderful three-piece ensemble that you could book," Anna offered with a smile.

Charlotte saw Dana glance at Pete, who made a slicing motion across his throat.

"You don't need to be so negative, Pete," Anna chided, resting Will on her shoulder. "A classical trio adds a level of sophistication to a wedding that makes it memorable. Dana, you shouldn't let Pete talk you into cutting corners on your special day."

"Hey, it's my special day too," Pete complained.

Anna ignored him. "You should try to make it as perfect and as memorable as you can."

Charlotte had to think back to Anna and Bill's wedding. No expense had been spared, and it definitely had been memorable. But she also knew that Anna had lost about ten pounds from the stress of trying to achieve perfection.

"Thanks for the offer, Anna," Dana said. "But I think we'll go with a pianist instead."

Anna gave a delicate shrug, as if to say *I tried*, just as her son let out a very loud burp.

"Hannah, would you mind helping me pass around the cake and goodies?" Charlotte asked, getting up from her chair.

Hannah followed her and took the plates out of the cupboard. "He's an adorable baby," Hannah said, setting the plates out on the counter. "You must be so thrilled."

Charlotte pulled the cake out of the refrigerator and pushed the door closed with her foot. "I'm happy for Anna and Bill and yes, I couldn't be happier with my brood. Six grandchildren. God is good."

"And three of each," Hannah added. She shot a quick glance toward the living room and lowered her voice. "Have you heard anything more from Kevin? Has he said what he's going to do about the children?"

Charlotte shook her head. "We'll just have to wait and see what happens."

"You can't simply let him waltz in and take your grandchildren away from you," Hannah said, her voice tinged with surprising anger.

"I doubt he can," Charlotte said.

"But are you certain?" Hannah lifted one eyebrow in question, and the beginnings of doubt roiled in Charlotte's midsection.

"Have you talked to your lawyer yet?" Hannah said. "I'm sure he'll give you good advice. He'll help you fight for the kids, which is what you should have done the first time around."

But a fight was exactly what Charlotte had hoped to avoid. The lawyer had been so certain that Kevin had limited rights where the children were concerned. However, Kevin seemed to be just as certain that he did have rights.

"He's out of town right now; I left a message for him to call me."

"You make sure you follow up on this, Charlotte. Don't let Kevin make all the decisions."

"When Bob and I decided not to pursue our own claim, it was because I wanted the children to feel they have some control over their lives," Charlotte said, concentrating on cutting the layer cake into precise triangles. "We prayed about it, and I have to believe that we made the right decision at that time. I'm going to talk to the lawyer and find out what our options are. But if Kevin is going to force our hand, well, then we'll have to rethink our situation."

She felt Hannah's hand on her shoulder. "I'm sorry, Charlotte. It's just I hate to see him get what he wants just because he wants it. He hasn't been a part of these children's lives ... and he left Denise all alone."

Charlotte clenched the knife a little harder and laid it down. "I know all that, Hannah," she said, turning to her friend. "But I also have to trust that God will show us what we should do."

Hannah gave her a quick hug, and once again Charlotte was thankful for the support of their friends.

Then, as Hannah pulled back, her attention was drawn away from Charlotte. "Looks like you've got another guest." Hannah pointed her chin toward the window by the kitchen table and, puzzled, Charlotte looked out.

Her heart fell.

A huge, bright red truck was pulling up beside Rosemary's car.

"Oh my," Hannah said, her dismay echoing Charlotte's own feelings as they watched Kevin step out of the truck. "I didn't think you would invite him."

"I didn't," Charlotte said, wondering what he was up to now. "He wasn't supposed to come until five." And it was only two now.

He carried a box wrapped in blue paper. How had he found out about the gathering today? Judging from the gift he carried, he seemed to know it was for Anna and Bill's baby boy.

The back porch door swung open, and Kevin strode into the house as if he were a regular visitor. "Hello, the house," he called out, bold as could be, setting the gift on the kitchen table.

Charlotte glanced toward the living room and saw every head spin around, looking toward the kitchen.

Emily was frowning and Sam looked surprised, but Christopher jumped to his feet and came running to his father. "You came!" he exclaimed, joy filling his voice. "You came!"

Charlotte glanced from her grandson to Kevin, who was bending over to give him a hug.

"I sure did, buddy. I'm glad you invited me to the party."

Charlotte struggled to keep her astonishment from showing. Christopher had invited Kevin? When? How?

Kevin straightened and turned to Charlotte. "So, here I am again," he said with a grin that seemed to expect that she would share his enthusiasm.

Charlotte could only stare.

Hannah, bless her heart, graciously intervened. "Kevin. Would you like some coffee? Or some punch?"

"Coffee would be great," Kevin said, rubbing his hands together as he shivered. "Still can't get used to this Nebraska winter." He gave Charlotte a grin. "I guess I should congratulate you. Another grandson." Then he looked down at Christopher, who was beaming up at him as if he were the boy's new, best friend. Kevin ruffled the top of Christopher's head. "Though I doubt he'll ever be as great a kid as this one."

Charlotte, still speechless at both Kevin's audacity and the plans Christopher had made without consulting them, couldn't even muster a polite smile.

"Where are my other kids?" Kevin said, grabbing his gift and striding down the hall and into the living room, seemingly oblivious to Charlotte's lack of welcome. "Hey, Emily. Sam. Come give your old man a hug."

Emily slowly got to her feet and walked over to him, Sam following behind.

Kevin enveloped Emily in an awkward hug but Sam hung back.

"Too big for that?" Kevin said, reaching over to grab Sam's hand.

Sam looked as if he was going to pull his hand back, but then at the last second allowed his father to shake his hand.

"Hey there," Sam said.

"Congratulations," Kevin said to Anna. "Can I have a look at the kid?"

"His name is Will."

"Very sorry. I didn't know what you named him." Kevin flashed her a crooked grin. For a split second, Charlotte saw what her daughter had seen in this man. Confidence, good looks, and a smattering of charm.

"But I did bring a present," he said, holding out the brightly wrapped gift.

"And what did you write on the card?" Anna's gaze ticked over the present, but she didn't take it. "Baby boy Stevenson? Or didn't you know his last name either?" Anna asked, her tone so frosty, Charlotte was surprised that she couldn't see her daughter-in-law's breath.

Kevin looked taken aback. "Hey. I just found out about this gig yesterday."

Anna just looked at him, one eyebrow lifted ever so slightly. "Gig?"

Kevin shrugged. "Well, okay. Party. Shindig. Get-together. Call it what you want."

"I thought you weren't supposed to come until five," Emily said, sitting beside Dana.

"Well, yeah, but then Christopher invited me here. So I thought, when this deal is done, we could head out."

"You can't take Emily and Christopher and Sam until after they take me and Madison tubing," Jennifer piped up.

Kevin looked over at her, frowning. "Why would you want to do that?"

Jennifer rolled her eyes. "Because it's fun, silly," she said with exaggerated disdain.

"Jennifer," Bill spoke up. "Watch your tone."

"Well, he's kind of silly if he doesn't think tubing is fun."

"Jennifer." Bill's tone meant business, and his daughter pulled her lips into a pout but said nothing more.

An awkward silence followed her outburst as Charlotte and Hannah returned to the kitchen to serve the cake.

"Kevin, what have you been doing the past few years?" Bill asked.

"Working on construction jobs. I was out on the West Coast for a long time. Then I got some work overseas for a few months. Afghanistan, mainly."

"That's kind of dangerous, isn't it?"

"Well, yeah. I had a few close calls," Kevin said with a note of pride. He launched into a story about his exploits, seeming to relish the details of the risks of the job. When he was done, he glanced around the room, almost as if he were expecting applause for his derring-do.

"My dad is really brave," Christopher piped up. "He told me that once he had to work on a building while rockets were going off."

And where had he heard that? Charlotte wondered as she passed the cake around. As far as she knew the children had had only the one visit with Kevin. Had Kevin been seeing the children after school after all?

"Rockets? And this is suitable work for a father of three children . . . how?" Anna asked, shifting Will onto her lap. She again arched one perfectly plucked eyebrow at Kevin.

To Charlotte's surprise, Kevin shifted in his chair. "It pays really good."

"Because money is so very important to children."

"It can't hurt," Kevin retorted, but Charlotte could see

that he didn't quite know what to say to Anna. "But I quit the overseas gig. I'm a father, and I know my responsibilities. I'm working closer to home now."

"I'm pleased to hear that you've belatedly discovered that," Anna said, her tone sounding anything but pleased.

"Aunt Anna, why are you talking like that to my dad?" Christopher asked, puzzled. "You sound mad at him."

Time to intervene. "Pete, why don't you and Sam take the children out for that ride on the snowmobile," Charlotte said, reaching toward Jennifer and Madison. "Christopher, you can help me get Madison and Jennifer ready."

"They're not babies," he said, still a bit put out by Anna's cross-examination of his father. "And I want to stay with my dad."

Charlotte was puzzled herself, wondering where this sudden allegiance to a man he barely knew had come from. Once the children were outside and occupied, she would have to get what information she could from Kevin.

"You can see him later, and I think the girls would like it better if you went along," she said, injecting a bright and cheerful tone into her voice.

Emily and Sam scrambled to their feet, seemingly glad for the escape, and Pete was right behind them. "Dana, you come too," he said.

Dana glanced around, as if unsure of her position in the family.

"Please, go ahead," Charlotte urged her, sensing her discomfort with the current situation. "Pete needs someone to keep things under control," she said with a smile.

In no time everyone was dressed in snow gear, and Pete led the charge outside, with Emily holding Madison's hand and Sam grabbing Jennifer's. Only Christopher seemed reluctant to leave, but he eventually followed them to the garage where the snowmobile was stored.

"Be careful," Charlotte reminded them as their excited chatter drifted back to her.

She waited a moment, making sure they were gone, and returned to the uncomfortable atmosphere that had pervaded the living room. Anna was rocking Will, and Bill was examining his hands. Rosemary was showing Hannah the children's stockings, and Bob and Frank sat in their respective chairs, their arms crossed.

Kevin, seemingly oblivious, finished off his cake, licked the fork, and set the plate aside. "That was great, Charlotte. I haven't had homemade cake in years."

"Does anyone want more coffee?" Charlotte asked, glancing around the room.

With no takers, she had no choice but to sit down beside Kevin. The conversation between Rosemary and Hannah faded away, and a heavy silence filled the room.

"Kevin, when are you going back to work?" Bill asked finally.

"Trying to get rid of me?" Kevin joked, but no one even cracked a smile.

"Just curious."

"Well, a lot of that depends . . ." He let the sentence drift away, and a chill shivered down Charlotte's spine.

"Depends on what?" Anna asked, her blue eyes like chips of ice.

Kevin lifted one hand in a vague gesture. "On what happens with the kids."

"And what is supposed to happen with the kids?" Anna asked, her hand patting Will's back and increasing its tempo.

"Why don't I take Will," Charlotte said, walking over to her obviously agitated daughter-in-law.

"Well, I figured that because I'm their dad . . . I have some rights."

Charlotte gently pulled Will out of Anna's hands and shot her a warning glance. She didn't want to antagonize Kevin, and Anna seemed especially agitated.

"You may be their father, but that doesn't make you their dad," Anna snapped, oblivious to Charlotte's concern. "It takes commitment to be a real parent. You've just popped into their lives and expect that you can simply pick up where you left off? It doesn't work that way, mister."

"Anna . . ." Bill laid his hand on her shoulder, but she shook it off.

"Who are you to come in here and mess up their lives?"

Kevin glared back at her. "And who are you to tell me what to do with my own children?"

"I'm their *aunt*," Anna said, putting extra emphasis on the last word. "And I've seen what these kids have had to deal with. It's been hard, and Bob and Charlotte have sacrificed a lot to take care of them, and they've done an amazing job. You think you can just take off when things aren't working and waltz back into their lives, throw around a bunch of money, and you're suddenly a dad?"

Kevin simply stared at Anna, his mouth silently working, as if he didn't know what to say first.

"Anna, would you like a cup of tea?" Bill asked, placing his hand on her shoulder again and squeezing. "Or maybe should we go for a walk?"

Anna spun around and glared at her husband. Bill looked down at her, and Charlotte could see Anna's face relax.

"Sorry," she said, her gaze ticking over everyone in the room. "I said too much. I'll blame it on hormones."

"Obviously," Kevin said, sounding relieved that he was off the hook. "Having a baby can do that to a woman. I remember Denise used to get real snarky..."

"I think that's enough, Kevin." Bob's voice was quiet, but the authority in it caught everyone's attention.

Kevin sensed it too and stopped what he was saying. He ran his hands up and down his legs as he looked at the floor.

The lights of the Christmas tree in the corner twinkled away, serene and complacent, and Charlotte felt a twinge of melancholy. Her visions of this Christmas had never included the precarious emotions that were churning in her stomach right now.

She cuddled Will closer, thankful for the soft warmth of his presence as she racked her brain, trying to think of something, anything to break the tension that had built in the room.

"Are you and Frank doing anything special this Christmas?" Charlotte asked Hannah, shooting a pleading glance to her friend to help her out.

Hannah blinked, as if trying to gather her own thoughts, and shook her head. "No. Nothing special, though I did volunteer us to go caroling at Bedford Gardens this year. Are you and Bob coming as well?"

"I don't sing," Bob grumped.

Hannah gave him a playful poke. "Oh, I've heard you in church. You have a great singing voice."

"I'll be there, Hannah," Charlotte chimed in.

She could hear Frank and Bill talking football across the room, and she hoped this might turn the conversation in a more neutral direction.

But all the while, Charlotte was acutely aware of Kevin sitting beside her, his face composed in a brittle mask. She wondered what he was thinking. What he was planning.

Then he glanced at his watch and got up. "Sorry to run, but I've got to do a few things." He glanced at Charlotte. "I'll be back for the kids at five sharp."

Charlotte simply nodded. When he left, it felt as if a huge weight had slipped off her shoulders.

No one said anything until a few minutes after the door closed behind him. Charlotte adjusted the blankets around Will and then got up and watched through the window to see if the children were anywhere in the yard while Kevin got in his truck and drove away. She didn't want them to think he was abandoning them.

Thankfully they weren't anywhere to be seen.

"I can't believe the gall of that man," Anna was saying as Charlotte returned to her seat. "And no, Bill, I won't be quiet. I probably shouldn't have attacked him like that, but he made me so angry."

Charlotte was surprised at her daughter-in-law. She was defending Sam, Emily, and Christopher with a ferocity she usually reserved for her own children.

Anna turned to Charlotte. "What are you and Bob going to do about this? Surely you can't just let him come and get the kids whenever he wants?"

Charlotte glanced at Bob, who was talking to Frank about crops; she sighed. "We haven't had a lot of time to figure out what to do. We're waiting to hear from the lawyer, but in the meantime, for the sake of the children, I don't want to limit access."

Anna sighed, folding her hands tightly together, shaking her head. "I'm convinced if he had even an inkling of what it cost to raise a child, he would run like the coyote he is."

In spite of the tension that had gripped everyone in the room, Charlotte had to smile. "Interesting analogy," Charlotte said with a teasing note in her voice.

Anna nodded, as if to emphasize her statement.

"Anyway, I'd like to thank everyone for coming and for your lovely gifts," Anna said, glancing around the room. "It was very kind of you."

Her polite thank-you was greeted with smiles and murmured replies. Though Anna spoke graciously, Charlotte couldn't help feel a small niggle of melancholy at the general quality of Anna's thank-yous. Charlotte had thought the moments she spent with Anna in the hospital had created a special bond. She had thought, at the very least, Anna would have acknowledged Charlotte's work in putting on this party.

But on the heels of that thought came a reprimand. She hadn't done this for recognition, Charlotte reminded herself. She had done it as a celebration. And it had been.

Chapter Seventeen

"What do you think of this for Arielle?" Sam asked Emily, holding up a golden chain with a filigree heart at the end.

The relentless Christmas music piped throughout the mall, the tacky decorations, and the endless streams of people carrying bags all were getting on Emily's nerves. They had only been there half an hour, and she was already getting tired. Of course it didn't help that the whole way here, their dad had been going on and on about how the family didn't realize he was serious. That he really cared for them and that he wanted to be a father to them.

If he really cared and wanted to be a father, you'd think he would have come up with something more original than another trip to the mall, Emily thought.

At least she had a chance to finish up some shopping.

She thought of the list she had in her pocket. The list with Ashley's name on it. She had known for a while what she was going to get her friend, but after the phone call yesterday she doubted she would be getting a present from Ashley this Christmas. At the same time she knew she was going to buy Ashley one anyhow.

But for now she had promised Sam she'd help him find a present for Arielle.

Emily reached over and turned over the tiny slip of paper attached to the necklace and gasped at the price. "Yikes, mister. Can you afford this?"

Sam sighed and gave it back to the man behind the counter. "Not really."

"We do have a convenient payment plan," the man offered, his smile as shiny as his face in the bright lights of the store.

"Do you really want to go there?" Emily asked. "You need to save up for college, and you don't get that many hours at the airport."

"I know. I know." Sam shoved his hands in the pockets of his pants. "Thanks anyway," he said to the store clerk. Then he turned and slouched away from the store. Emily followed him.

"Look, Sam, you don't have to blow your budget to get her a present," she said. "Buy her something simple. Girls appreciate that."

Sam sighed and shook his head. "Like you appreciated that camera Dad bought for you?"

Emily felt a burst of shame. "I didn't know if I should say no to him."

"Yeah, I know what you mean." Sam glanced down the length of the mall, as if looking for their father and brother. "Christopher sure seems to be all over Dad."

"I know. And it bugs me." Emily stopped and dropped onto an empty bench, blowing out a sigh that poofed up her bangs. Sam sat down beside her, his elbows hanging on his knees. "What do you think is going on? Grandma and Grandpa haven't said much."

"I don't dare ask Dad, because you know what? I don't wanna know. And Grandma and Grandpa seem to be laying low. Last night I tried to talk to Grandma about Dad, and all she said was that it was good that he was back in our lives. Which tells me nothing." Emily stared at the store ahead of them, seeing but not noticing the fancy clothes on display.

On the way here their father had promised they could pick out their Christmas present. They could get whatever they wanted. Snowboards, stereos, new cell phones—didn't matter.

"What are you going to ask Dad to buy you for Christmas? That sweet snowboard at Sled and Shred?"

Sam slowly shook his head. "I don't think so. It seems kind of greedy and I don't want a big expensive present from him, you know?" He glanced over at Emily, his dark hair falling into his eyes. "I guess I had hoped that we could just be doing things together, not going out for fancy dinners and then going to the mall."

"I know. It seems lame to come here again. I had way more fun tubing this afternoon with Uncle Pete and Miss Simons than I'm having on this dream shopping trip." Emily shivered. "I can't believe I just said that."

Sam poked her. "I can't either."

"And if we come home with more stuff, I feel like it's not fair to Grandma and Grandpa. Because whatever Dad gets us, I know they couldn't afford it."

Sam laughed a bit. "Last year we got those stockings,

remember? I'm sure they didn't cost anywhere near what one of Christopher's Nintendo games did."

"But I like my stocking."

"I like mine too."

Emily swung her purse between her legs, watching it go back and forth. "This Christmas sure isn't turning out like I thought it would," she said with a heavy sigh, thinking not only of her father but of Ashley as well.

"No kidding."

Emily paused a moment, wondering if she should say it. "Do you think Dad wants us to move in with him?"

"Move into what? His motel room?"

Emily shrugged. "Maybe he would buy a place." The words pushed into her mind as if demanding to be voiced. She took a breath, took a chance, and released them: "Would you move in with him if he did?"

For a moment Sam didn't respond, and she wondered if he had heard her. She felt as if she were teetering on the edge of a frightening, yet at the same time interesting, place. What would happen if she took that step? How much would change?

Then Sam shook his head. "I don't know. I kind of doubt it."

Emily released her pent-up breath. She hadn't even realized she'd been holding it in.

Sam glanced at her. "What about you? Would you move?"

Emily sighed, still swinging her purse. "Sometimes I feel like I want to get away from everyone and everything. Especially after Ashley's weird behavior around Ryan."

"You two still fighting?"

Emily shrugged. "Not really, but I've been waiting for her to make the next move."

"Would you go?"

"I don't know. I kind of feel like I'm at home at the farm."

"I know what you mean. In a way, I don't want things to change anymore. I feel like I'm finally getting my balance. And now, all of a sudden I feel like everywhere I turn, I'm looking at change again, what with Dad showing up, and trying to plan my future, and . . ." Sam pursed his lips, staring ahead.

"Your college applications?" Emily finished the sentence for him.

Sam nodded, rocking just a bit. "Yeah. That. Arielle knows exactly what she wants, but I don't. I'm not even sure I want to go to school."

"What else would you do? Work construction like Dad?" Emily said the words like a joke, but at the same time she was a bit worried about her big brother.

"I don't think so," Sam said. "Though it'd be nice to have a bunch of money to throw around. I could buy Arielle that necklace."

Emily watched the people streaming past them, all carrying bags, most of them hurrying. Most of them looking tense.

Grandma always said money didn't buy happiness, but Emily had never truly believed it. Until their dad came into their lives. Now she finally had the camera she'd always dreamed of. And right now her dad was encouraging her to buy just about anything she wanted. And here she was, in the middle of an awesome mall, sitting on a bench with her brother. Her dad's money wasn't making her feel very happy. If anything, it was making her feel mixed-up.

"I don't think Arielle cares what you get her, Sam," Emily said. "I don't think money is important to her."

"How do you know?"

Emily gave her brother a quick sideways glance. "Because if I had a boyfriend I wouldn't care what kind of present he got me. I'd just be glad that he thought of me."

She was grateful Sam didn't laugh at her. When she took a chance and looked at him again, he wasn't looking at her like she was some big dummy.

"You really think so?"

Emily held his gaze. "I know so."

"Okay, so what should I do? Because I'm not meeting up with Dad until I have something for Arielle. Last time we were here, he wanted to pay for whatever I wanted to get her, and no way I'm doing that."

Emily focused on the store windows she'd been staring at mindlessly for the past few minutes; then she got up. "I think I have the perfect gift," she said, walking toward the nearest store. "Buy that scarf on that mannequin." Emily pointed to a deep green-and-gold scarf she knew would go great with a sweater Arielle had. "And use it to wrap up a box of chocolates."

Sam looked thoughtful and grinned. "Sounds really good."

"Trust me. It's perfect. Not too much, yet kind of neat—thoughtful but not expensive." From the way Sam was smiling, Emily knew she had just taken one more load off her brother's mind.

And she knew what to get Ashley as well.

Ten minutes later they phoned their dad and headed out to meet him and Christopher, pushing through crowds of people and avoiding women pushing baby buggies loaded with kids and shopping bags.

"What are we going to do about the presents Dad wants us to pick out?" Emily asked, sidestepping a woman dragging two crying children.

"I dunno. I don't feel right about getting more. I think we should just tell him that the stuff we got the first time is enough." Sam sighed, and Emily knew exactly how he felt.

They took a shortcut through the crowded food court and met up with their dad and Christopher by the ice cream stand.

"Did you see anything you liked?" their dad asked them when he saw them coming.

Emily glanced at Sam, who gave their dad one of his signature shrugs. Their dad looked over at her, and she gave him a quick smile. "I couldn't make up my mind."

"I saw a purse store that you might like to check out," their dad said.

"I found a cool shop that sells snowboards," Christopher piped up. "I saw one that you would like, Sam. I told Dad he should buy it for you, but he wanted you to pick it out."

Sam shuffled his feet, pushing a candy wrapper along the floor of the mall with the toe of his sneaker. "I'm okay. I don't need a snowboard. That iPod you bought me was enough."

"But Christopher here says you love snowboarding. And skateboarding. We could get you a skateboard. They sell those at the shop too."

Whoa, their dad was really not playing fair, Emily thought as she saw Sam's head snap up at that. Sam loved snowboarding, but skateboarding was his passion.

But then Sam said, "I'm okay. Really."

"Oh, c'mon. I know there's all kinds of things you guys want." Their dad clapped Christopher on the shoulder. "This young fella has his present all picked out, so maybe we should go get his first."

Christopher held their dad's hand, and the way he looked up at him made Emily feel kind of weird. Like their dad was his best friend.

Then she remembered how Christopher had said he had invited his dad to come to the party for baby Will, and how she had overheard him talking to their dad on the telephone. Worry slithered around her stomach. What if Christopher wanted to go with their dad if he asked? Christopher had always worried that their dad had left because of him; now he was getting all kinds of their dad's attention. Would Christopher get pulled into that?

She pushed the unwelcome thought aside. She and Sam would have to talk to him, that's all. Try to explain that any decision they made, they would all make together.

But the way Christopher was looking at their dad right now, it would be hard to convince Christopher not to go with him.

"Chris decided he wants an PlayStation 5."

Sam frowned. "Are you sure, Christopher? We'd have to ask Grandma and Grandpa if you could hook it up to their television."

Their dad waved his hand. "No worries there—'cause

guess what else we're going to do?" His eager gaze raked over each of them.

"Guess, you guys," Christopher prompted, almost jumping up and down in delight.

"I don't know," Sam said.

"We're also going to buy all of you your own flat-screen television to share," their dad announced.

Was he kidding?

"But we can only get farmer vision," Emily said.

Their dad frowned. "What do you mean, farmer vision?"

"We only get the channels you get through an antenna."

"No cable? Streaming?"

"Nope."

"Shoot. That's right. Well, then I guess you'll just be able to use the television for the PlayStation then," their dad said. "So let's go get that first."

Emily traded a puzzled look with Sam. How would they explain all this to Grandma and Grandpa? What would they say, and, even more important, how would they feel about all this stuff their dad was getting them and all the money he wanted to spend on them?

They ended up back at the store where they had gotten their other presents, and Christopher and their dad walked straight to the television section. The wall was a bank of televisions of every size, most of them huge, the same pictures of Santa Claus flickering on each one.

"We shouldn't get one too big," Christopher was saying.

Their dad put his hand on Christopher's shoulder. "What size do you think we should get, Sam?"

"We don't need to do this."

Emily could tell Sam felt uncomfortable being the one to make that decision. She saw the price tags on the televisions as well. She couldn't believe their dad would spend that much money on them. "I don't think we should do this either," she put in.

"C'mon, Chris wants one. How about this one?" Their dad pointed to a smaller LCD-screen television. "It's got a built-in DVD player. That way you guys can watch your own movies too. How cool is that?"

Actually, pretty cool, Emily thought, trying to imagine being able to watch their own movies without having Grandma and Grandpa complaining that they wanted to watch something else.

"Can you afford all this?" Sam finally asked.

"Hey, I'm a self-made man. I've got more than enough money, and I didn't have to go to school to make it." Their dad laughed. "What do you guys think?" Their dad glanced from Emily to Sam, but neither of them could say anything.

Emily saw her father frown; then his eyes seemed to sharpen. "C'mon you guys," he said, with another laugh that sounded forced this time. "I'm getting you guys some primo stuff here. The least you could do is be excited."

Emily felt like she was being ungrateful, but the size of the present still made her feel funny. She hardly knew her father, and now he had burst into their lives throwing money around.

But he was looking a bit ticked with them right now. "I guess it's cool," she said, pretending to be excited.

"Sam?"

"Yeah. Awesome."

"Okay. It's done. We'll get this. Chris, let's go over to the salesman and let him know that we want the television and a PS5."

"This is so cool. I can hardly wait to tell Dylan." Christopher danced alongside their father, his cheeks flushed and his eyes sparkling with excitement.

Emily waited till their dad was a ways away; then she asked Sam. "Is he kidding?"

"I guess not. But Christopher seems excited and, well..."

"I know," Emily said with a sigh. "I don't want to be the one to ruin his fun. Still, how are we going to explain this to Grandma and Grandpa?"

Sam just shrugged and followed Christopher and their dad to the counter. One of the sales clerks was dispatched to get the television, and their dad pulled out his wallet, snapping his credit card down on the counter.

"I'll put it on this one," he said.

The clerk swiped it, frowned, and swiped it again.

"Here's the PS5." When one of the clerks set the shiny, plastic-wrapped box on the counter, even Emily's heart did a little flip. To just be able to choose something that expensive without having to wait and save up for it ... it boggled her mind.

"I'm sorry, sir, but this card has been declined." The cashier handed their dad the card back.

"That's impossible. Try again," their dad said.

He did and shook his head again. "Sorry. Still declined."

"What does *declined* mean?" Christopher asked, his eyes on the PS5.

"Doesn't matter. I have another card." Their dad looked mad. He opened his wallet and flipped through all the cards, but it looked like he couldn't find the one he needed. He opened the cash part of his wallet and flipped through all the bills there. It looked like a lot, but when he shoved the wallet back in his pocket, Emily assumed it wasn't enough.

He stood there a moment, his hands on his hips. "Okay. Okay. I have to make a call," he said. He pointed to the kids. "Just stay here." He pulled his phone out of his pocket and dialed as he walked a short distance away.

From where they stood, Emily could see that he was getting angry. He turned away from them, but his voice grew louder. Finally he snapped the phone shut and came back. He was smiling but it looked completely fake.

"Well, I guess we'll have to come back on Monday with my other credit card to pay for this," he said, unable to look them in the eye. "It seems there's some miscommunication between the bank and my credit card company. We should probably go."

"But what about the PlayStation? And the television?" Christopher asked. "Aren't we getting them?"

"Another time," their dad said, taking him by the arm.

"But I thought we were going to get them today." Christopher, getting pulled along by his dad, looked longingly back over his shoulder at the boxes being removed from the counter.

"No. We're not. Now stop going on about it. We have to go."

The disappointment on Christopher's face and the way their father was treating him made Emily upset. How could he build him up and then let him down like that?

"I really wanted a PS5," Christopher said.

Their dad gave Christopher's arm a rough shake. "Stop whining, Chris."

Emily caught up to their dad at the same time Sam did, suddenly angry. It wasn't Christopher's fault, yet their dad acted like it was. "It's okay, Christopher," Emily said. Then she turned to her dad, holding his gaze. "And his name is not Chris."

Their dad frowned. "What did you say to me?"

Emily felt her heart pound as their father glared at her. She hadn't meant to say the words out loud, but she had. Now her father was angry with her.

But as he stared her down, she remembered talking to Ashley about standing up to Ryan's sister. And she thought about how Anna's mom had pushed her around and how Grandma had apologized for not standing up to her.

Sometimes grown-ups are wrong, she remembered Grandma saying. And this time, she knew her father was wrong.

"You don't need to get angry at him because of your mistake," she said, trying to sound quiet and firm at the same time. The way Grandma sometimes did when she was dealing with unreasonable people. "It wasn't his fault."

Their dad looked angry and Emily experienced a genuine flash of fear.

Then, just as quickly as his anger had come, it disappeared again. "You're right," he said, lifting his hands, palms up. "I'm sorry. It's just that I was so excited to get you guys some nice stuff and then, to have that mess-up with the credit card... But I'll get it straightened up in the morning, and I can get you guys here tomorrow."

"We've got church tomorrow," Sam said.

"Right. Right."

"And I think we're okay with the presents you already gave us," Emily added, feeling a bit more confident after her dad's apology. "We really don't want you to spend any more money on us."

"But I want to. And I easily can. I've got lots of room on the other card. Lots of money yet." Then their dad's expression turned kind of funny, and he gave a laugh that wasn't really a laugh. "I've never had much money; I certainly didn't when you guys were growing up. Now I really, really want to make it up to you. I'm making good money now, for the first time in my life, and I want to show you that I love you."

He sounded sincere, but Emily still felt a bit funny about the whole situation.

Money can't buy love. Grandma said that lots, and it was as if Emily now heard those words from a different place in her life. Now it was as if she understood them on a different level.

For just a flash, she felt sorry for her dad.

"What do we do now?" their dad asked.

"Maybe we should go home." Emily was getting used to this taking-charge business. "It's late, and we have church tomorrow."

Their father nodded and led them out of the mall to the truck. He didn't say anything more about buying them a Christmas present, and the trip home was quiet.

Christopher sat beside Emily in the back seat of the truck this time instead of in front with their dad—as if he didn't trust his dad as much anymore.

Sam sat where Christopher had been sitting.

They pulled into the driveway, and when their dad had parked his truck, he turned around, facing them all at the same time. "I'm sorry things turned out the way they did," he said. "I really want to get you guys that stuff, okay? Maybe another time?"

This netted him another nod. It was as if no one knew quite what to say.

"Tell your grandma I'd like to come and pick you guys up on Monday after school."

Sam nodded. "I'll tell her," he said.

Sam then got out of the front of the truck and, to Emily's surprise, opened the back door for her.

"Bye, sport," their dad said to Christopher, but the boy's only response was a quick wave as he followed Emily out of the vehicle. Their dad waited until they got to the house; then he backed out of the driveway, his taillights winking in the dark, the noise of his truck slowly fading away behind the snow-covered trees lining the road.

"Why was Dad so mad at me?" Christopher asked, still watching the driveway. "It wasn't my fault we didn't get the PS5."

Emily heard Sam muttering something about him being a jerk; she hoped Christopher didn't hear that. "I think he felt embarrassed," Emily said.

"Well, he didn't need to yell at me. I'm tired of people yelling at me." Christopher pulled away from Emily. "I thought he was my friend, but our dad got mad at me too. I don't do anything wrong, and people get mad at me. Sometimes I wish I could just run away. I wanted to live with Dad, like he asked me to, but now I don't want to anymore."

Emily felt like someone had just shoved a splinter of ice into her heart. Their dad had asked Christopher to live with him? What was he trying to do, break up their family?

"What are you talking about?" Sam asked, his face like a mask, his breath wreathing around his head. Emily could see the glitter in his eyes and knew he was angry but trying not to show it. "When did Dad ask you to live with him?"

Christopher glanced from Sam to Emily, a stubborn look on his face. "When I phoned him. Yesterday."

"You've been talking to him on the phone?" Sam asked, shoving his hands in his pockets and hunching his shoulders against the cold.

"He said I could call whenever I wanted." Christopher swiped his mittened hand over his face and sniffed. "And then he asked me if I wanted to live with him."

Sam pulled in a slow breath, and Emily crouched down on the snow-covered driveway beside her little brother. She was cold and tired. She could smell the smoke from the corn burner and knew that Grandma and Grandpa would have hot chocolate and cookies waiting for them. As she glanced at the rectangle of gold light shining out from the house, she wanted nothing more than to be inside, where it was safe and comfortable and familiar. But they had to get this taken care of before they went into the house.

Like she had done with Sam, she voiced the question she knew hovered in each of their minds: "Do you *want* to live with our dad, Christopher?" she asked.

Christopher sniffed again. "I don't know. I thought I did, but he got mad at me too, like everyone else. I just don't want people to be mad at me. To think I'm a silly little kid."

"No one is mad at you." *Except our father*, Emily thought, feeling a spurt of anger again herself. "And no one thinks you're a silly little kid."

"Yes. They do. Sam got mad at me about writing on his stupid papers. I was just trying to help Uncle Pete with the house plans, but he didn't want my help. He was just humoring me, and I know that means he was just trying to make me feel good. He's not going to build a house, and he's not going to use my plans."

"You shouldn't feel bad about Uncle Pete," Emily said, trying to vouch for their uncle. "I'm sure he thought your plans were great, but building a house is a big decision for him and Dana, and they probably don't quite know what to do yet."

Christopher blinked and seemed to consider that information. "You mean maybe he thought my plans were good?"

"I'm sure he did." Emily squeezed her little brother's shoulder. Christopher gave her a wavering smile and swiped at his face again.

Emily gave him a quick hug. "And I know that no one thinks you're silly, even if we aren't always nice to you."

Then Sam came over to Christopher and knelt down in the snow beside his little brother. "Hey, Christopher, I know I haven't been the best brother to you, but there's so much stuff going on for me, and so many big decisions I have to make. I shouldn't have yelled at you. I'm sorry."

"It's okay." Christopher looked at him and took in a breath. "I just don't like it when we fight. It makes my stomach hurt."

His comment made Emily uncomfortable. Did Ashley feel the same way?

Christopher sniffed again as Emily pushed herself to her feet and brushed the melting snow off the knees of her blue jeans. "Now, let's see if Grandma has some hot chocolate for us."

"I hope she has some cookies too," Christopher said.

"The way she's been baking lately, I'm sure there're lots of cookies." Sam clapped his hand on his brother's shoulder and Emily took Christopher's hand.

"And cake," Emily said, wondering how to avoid the temptation of all those goodies.

They walked together to the house, and as soon as they were inside Emily went straight to the phone. Ashley was her friend, and in spite of the mistakes she had made, Emily knew she wanted to stay friends.

When Ashley answered the phone, the happiness in her voice made Emily realize she had done the right thing.

Chapter Eighteen

"Got the mail," Bob said, tossing the envelopes on the table. He blew his nose, and started ripping open the envelopes while Charlotte finished wiping down the kitchen counters. The dishwasher chugged away, and the washing machine was going through its fourth load of laundry.

"Anything interesting?" Charlotte asked, wiping her hands.

"A bunch of Christmas cards and some flyers, bills, and junk mail." Bob sat down and began sorting through the pile of mail. "Can't believe how quick the mailbox fills up this time of the year. But the bills keep coming. I sometimes wonder how we're ever going to afford everything that's coming up."

"We're not doing that badly," Charlotte said.

Bob shrugged. "No, but it's surprising how quick the money comes and goes—mostly goes."

Charlotte had to think of Pete and his worries; she wondered if he had ever said anything to Bob.

"We've got a few expenses coming up, that's for sure," Charlotte said, edging gently toward the topic she wanted to discuss.

"Yeah. Where Pete and Dana are going to live for one," Bob said.

"You haven't talked to him about that yet, have you?" Charlotte said, thinking of how despondent Pete had been just a few days ago when he talked to her about his living arrangements.

Bob shook his head as he tossed aside a couple of pieces of junk mail. "Been waiting for him to bring it up."

Men, Charlotte thought with a flush of frustration. "And what if he's waiting for you to bring it up?"

Bob glanced up at her and frowned. "It's his future. He should be making his own plans and discussing them with me. I shouldn't have to be the one nagging him."

Charlotte had to smile. "You think Pete and Dana would be able to build a house?"

"As long as it's not too fancy, we'll find a way to make it work." Bob sighed and shook his head. "There's a nice piece of land on the other side of the creek that might be perfect for them. It can all work out; we just need to make some plans, that's all. Besides, I certainly don't want them both living in the spare room after they're married."

Charlotte smiled, knowing she would have to do a bit of motherly interfering. At the same time, she felt another burden slip off her shoulders.

And Pete's.

Then Charlotte saw the corner of a cream-colored envelope peeking out from behind a store flyer and pulled it out. When she glanced at the return address her heart missed its next beat, and she dropped into the nearest chair.

Bob glanced up from the envelope he was ripping open. "What's wrong?"

Charlotte handed him the envelope, and his face grew hard. "Lewiston, Anders, and Rochester," he read, "attorneys at law." He shook his head and tore it open. "One guess as to where this comes from."

Charlotte fidgeted in her chair while Bob pulled the heavy paper out of the envelope and skimmed the letter, his mouth moving as he read the words.

Then he scratched his temple with one rough forefinger and dropped the letter on the table.

"Well, it seems that Kevin has hired a lawyer to represent him in the matter of the guardianship of Sam, Emily, and Christopher Slater."

Charlotte's breath caught in her throat. "He's going through with his plans."

Bob blew out a sigh. "I guess."

"What do we do? I'm still waiting for that lawyer to call back. He said he would be back by the middle of this week. Should we get someone else? I didn't think Kevin had any rights where the children were concerned..." Charlotte got up and lifted the phone. "I can call another lawyer. I knew I should have done what Melody suggested I do. I knew I should have pushed to get firm custody."

"Sit down, Charlotte. Don't call another lawyer yet."

"But we have to fight him." A thread of panic wound itself around Charlotte's heart. "We have to stop him. He can't just come into the children's lives and upset everything, ruin all the hard work we've done."

"I think we should just hold off for now."

"For what?" Charlotte couldn't believe Bob was simply going to let Kevin rip their family apart.

"I'd prefer to see what he's going to do before we rattle his cage too hard."

As Charlotte held her husband's calm, steady gaze, her mind slipped back to the comment Bob had made before Kevin came into their lives. How sometimes he thought it was too much. Did he still feel that way?

"But we know what he's going to do," she said, struggling to keep her voice even, calm. "He wants to get guardianship of the children. He says it right there in the letter."

"I know, but I don't want to give him a reason to fight just for the sake of fighting." Bob leaned forward again and gave Charlotte a careful smile. "I'm as worried about what he's going to do as you are. I prefer not to make him think of the kids as just another possession, something to have just because someone else might want them more. Besides, we said we would pray about this, and we have. Maybe now it's time to leave things in God's hands."

Charlotte felt the sincerity in his voice as relief softened her bones. "You don't want him to have the children."

Bob's face grew hard and in that moment, she saw the quiet strength her husband possessed. "Of course not! He is not taking the children away from us; the only way that would happen is if that's what the children truly want."

"I'm scared they'll be seduced by all the good things he seems to be able to give them."

"Now, Charlotte, I think we've been doing a better job than that, and I know Denise did as well. Those kids aren't materialistic."

Maybe not, but Charlotte couldn't forget the way Christopher's eyes had shone when he showed her his gifts.

"We have to trust that God will give us wisdom to deal with Kevin in the right way," Bob continued.

Charlotte nodded. "I just wish I knew what that was. Everyone seems to be giving us such different advice; I don't know what to think anymore."

"Well, I do know we aren't playing his game. I'm not spending good money on a lawyer when I'm sure we can talk things out with him." He reached over and took the phone from her. He pulled a card out of his pocket. "Kevin's number," he said, when Charlotte shot him a puzzled frown.

He adjusted his glasses, tilted his head so he could see through his bifocals, and punched in the number. As he pushed his glasses up his nose, he winked at Charlotte.

How could he be so casual? Her heart was still thumping in her chest, remembering the words in the letter.

"Yes. Kevin. Good to talk to you too . . . Yes, we got the letter. Charlotte and I would like to talk to you . . . No, I don't think we need to do this with your lawyer present . . . It's just some arrangements we need to make for the children." Bob stopped, nodding his head. Listening. "I think we could avoid a lot of extra work and some money if we figure a few things out on our own before the lawyers get involved." He nodded again. "Why not right away? You can come here, and if the children want to go with you after school, we can discuss that with them when they come home."

Charlotte felt a jolt of dismay. How often was Kevin going to be having the children? He just saw them Saturday evening; now he wanted to see them again. She had her own plans and things she wanted to do with the children.

As soon as the thought was formulated, she tried to quash it. It wasn't about her or Bob or Kevin. It was about the children.

Bob made a few more arrangements and then hung up the phone. "He's coming right away," he said, drumming his fingers on the table.

Charlotte's heart started up again. *So soon?*

"But what are we going to say to him? Are you sure we shouldn't have some legal advice?" Charlotte asked, feeling breathless at the thought of actually confronting Kevin about the children.

"We already know we have good legal grounds for keeping the children, and we decided not to cement those legal grounds last year, right?" Bob leveled a questioning gaze at her.

"Yes."

"And we did that because our first concern was that we didn't want to cut off any recourse the children might have to make a decision about their father themselves, right?"

Charlotte nodded. "I know. But truth to tell, now I'm afraid."

Bob folded his hands together on the letter from Kevin's lawyer, his thick, work-roughened hands looking incongruous against the creamy linen of the stationery. Did they really have a chance, two ordinary people trying to do what was right, against a man who seemed to be thinking only of himself and his needs?

"I'm afraid too," Bob said quietly, rubbing one thumb over the other. "That's why, before we do anything, I want us to pray together."

Charlotte drew a steadying breath and nodded. Then she reached across the table and covered his callused hands with her own, feeling a touch of melancholy at the age spots starting to show on the backs of her hands, the lines of her raised veins, and the wrinkles in her once-smooth skin.

How can we go up against a young man with money and energy and unlimited hubris? We go in God's strength, she thought, lowering her head. *We go trusting that God will not do what is best for us, but what is best for the children.*

"Dear Lord," Bob began, his quiet voice resonating in the quiet of the kitchen. "We are troubled and tired, and we are faced with some big decisions. We want to put our problems in Your hands. We want You to help us make the best decisions for the children, and we pray that You will work in Kevin's heart to do the same. Help us, always, to lean on You and to realize that these children were Your children before they were ever ours."

Charlotte repeated Bob's last words in her mind as she clung to his hand. There were times she had to remind herself that the children were only hers and Bob's to care for, not to claim.

Yet each time she mentally struggled to relinquish her hold on them, she always felt as if she had to make one last, quick grab for them.

"Help us to leave them in Your hands," Bob said. "Give us wisdom to deal with Kevin, and help us to love him too." He paused for a moment, and then said, "Amen."

Charlotte repeated it, clinging to Bob's hand for just a moment longer. Then she got up and put the water on for coffee, pulled out a plate, and arranged some cookies on it, getting ready for their company. Busy work that kept her mind off what lay ahead of them.

Bob quietly sorted through the rest of the mail while Charlotte kept shooting anxious glances at the clock. She felt as if they were approaching a major turning point with Kevin, and she wasn't sure what Bob had in mind.

Finally, unable to keep her thoughts to herself another minute, she sat down beside her husband. He looked up from the farm paper he was reading, as if sensing she had something important to say.

"Awhile ago, you thought maybe having the children might be too much," Charlotte said, deciding to be direct. "Do you still think that?"

Bob rubbed his thumb over his whiskers, making a rasping noise in the quiet of the house. "There were times I thought that about our own children," he finally said. "It's a pretty normal reaction. I didn't really mean anything by it."

"You didn't?"

Bob waved her question away. "Of course not. It's just talk. Just thinking out loud."

Relief flickered through her. "I just wanted to make sure."

Bob leaned back in his chair, folding his hands over his stomach. "Just in case I was going to offer Kevin the kids—lock, stock, and barrel?"

"Well, no . . ."

"Admit it, Charlotte," Bob said with a laugh. "You've thought it."

Charlotte held his teasing gaze and replied with her own smile. "Okay. I'll admit it. There was a time when I wondered if you regretted taking in the children."

"Have you? Ever regretted taking them in?" Bob countered.

Charlotte let the question settle and then decided the absolute truth was the best. "Yes. There have been times."

"But they're still here, aren't they?"

"Yes."

Bob nodded, rocking in his chair. "Everyone is allowed a few second thoughts, Charlotte. It's not sinful to admit that there are times you wish life had turned out differently than it has. If I wondered sometimes whether we should have had our own children, it's natural to feel that way about taking in Denise's." Then his expression grew serious. "But just for the record, I'm thankful for Sam, Emily, and Christopher, and I wouldn't trade them for anything. You need to know that before we talk to Kevin, and you need to believe it."

His serious tone held her full attention. "Why do you say that?"

"Because when Kevin comes, I'm about to call his bluff."

The glint of sunlight reflecting off a windshield outside caught Charlotte's attention.

"Well, get ready. Because he's here." She wanted to ask Bob more, but Kevin was already walking toward the house.

Bob got up from the table and went to the family room. He gathered together a pad of paper, a couple of pencils, and a calculator. Charlotte wanted to ask him what he was doing, but Kevin was already inside the porch, calling out his greetings. To Charlotte's momentary annoyance, he sounded very comfortable. As if he stopped by on a regular basis.

"Hello, Charlotte," Kevin said as he entered the kitchen. "Bob."

Bob stood up and indicated the chair across the table. "Sit down, Kevin. Charlotte, you come sit down next to me."

Still mystified but trusting the glimmer she caught from Bob's eye, Charlotte did as she was told, but not before she put cookies on the table and poured everyone a cup of coffee. *Always the hostess*, she thought.

"So, what are we going to discuss?" Kevin asked, clasping his hands and resting his elbows on the table. His gaze flicked from Charlotte to Bob, his smile confident, even jaunty. As if he hadn't a care in the world.

"The care of the children," Bob said, picking up a pen. "You said you wanted to have custody of the children, and I can understand why. They've been a blessing to us, and we love them dearly, but at the same time, they're quite a lot of responsibility. Financial and otherwise."

Charlotte felt a jolt of horror at the blunt honesty of Bob's words, but his hand on her knee, under the table, made her trust her husband. So she said nothing.

"Of course. I get that. Kids cost money," Kevin agreed.

"With that in mind..." Bob pulled the pad of paper in front of him, the calculator within easy reach. "I thought I would let you know some of the expenses you'll need to be prepared for when and if you still want to take care of the children."

Bob ran the pencil down the pad, dividing it into four columns, and put a name above each—Sam, Emily, and Christopher, and above the last column he wrote "All."

"First of all, we've got the basic stuff, monthly groceries and that kind of thing." Bob glanced at Charlotte. "What do you figure the kids cost us per month for food?"

Charlotte finally realized what Bob was up to.

"Well, that's hard to say because we grow our own garden and milk our own cow," she said, "But if I had to buy all our food," she did some quick mental calculating and gave Bob a figure that he put under the All column.

"What about clothes?"

Charlotte gave him a rough figure for that, calculating in what the children spent on themselves. Sure, it came out of their allowance, but the allowance came from the farm account; so, in a way, it was their own expense anyway.

Kevin frowned. "Are you sure?"

Charlotte shrugged. "That's in Harding. I suppose it would cost a bit more if you lived near a larger city."

Kevin worked his lower lip, his eyes on the paper Bob had in front of him.

"Then we've got the potential for braces. So far Emily and Sam are okay, but we're not sure about Christopher." Bob scribbled another figure down under Christopher's name.

And so it went: transportation, school fees, incidentals, gifts, potential college funds, medical insurance, medical expenses. As Bob wrote it all down, Charlotte began to wonder herself how they managed to afford having the children.

When the money flowed in and out of the account,

she never thought to add it up. Now she knew why there were times they struggled to keep up. Yes, it all balanced in the long run, but seeing the costs laid out in black and white made her realize exactly how much taking care of children cost.

Obviously the figures were a revelation to Kevin too. He no longer leaned forward, his face creased in a confident smile. A hint of doubt had crept into his eyes, and he fingered his chin, as if considering what Bob had written down in front of him.

"Are you sure that's what it comes to?" he asked as Bob added the numbers in each column.

"If anything, I think we've been a bit conservative," Bob murmured, glancing from the calculator to the paper as he scribbled down one total. "And I haven't even added in the cost of either renting a place big enough for four people or the monthly payments on a house loan."

Kevin shoved his hand through his artfully tousled hair, rearranging its perfect spikes. "But surely there's got to be a way it costs less than that?"

Bob shrugged. "Not really." He added up the last figures and then added up each column. He wrote a final figure across the bottom of the page and underlined it twice, just in case Kevin should miss it.

Then he spun the pad of paper around and pushed it toward Kevin. "That's the yearly cost of having the children in your home. I've taken the liberty of putting down a monthly rental payment as an option in case you didn't want to make the commitment to purchasing a house. Renting is cheaper, but I would recommend, in the long run, buying a house. Just makes more sense from a financial point of view."

Kevin glanced over the numbers, pursed his lips, and slowly blew out his breath.

He looked scared, Charlotte thought.

And she didn't blame him. When she saw the final figure, she felt scared too. Did they really have to come up with that much money every year to take care of three extra children?

"You're absolutely certain about this?" Kevin asked, rubbing his chin with his thumb and forefinger. "You're not just playing dirty?"

Bob leaned forward. "Kevin, I don't play games. All I'm doing here is being realistic. Letting you know what you'd be taking on if you decided you wanted to have the children."

Kevin's gaze flicked from the paper to Charlotte to Bob. "How can you afford to do this? You're only farmers. I'm the one making the big money."

"It's a matter of priorities," Bob said, his voice quiet. "We choose what we spend our money on and budget accordingly."

Kevin folded his arms over his chest, his fingers tapping out a nervous beat on his arms. "Did you guys plan this to get me to change my mind? You don't want me to be involved in their lives, do you? You don't think I deserve them."

Charlotte waited a moment, trying to find exactly the right thing to say to the man who was the father of her grandchildren. "We don't deserve them either, Kevin," she said quietly. "But when they needed us we were there..."

"Meaning I wasn't."

"Meaning, we were available." Charlotte stopped there because, in one way, Kevin was right. He wasn't there when his family needed him the most, and on one level, he had to recognize that as well.

Kevin got up and grabbed the back of the chair, clenching and unclenching it with his hands. "I'll get another job." He spun around, walked away from the table and then returned. "A better-paying job."

"You've moved around a lot, Kevin," Bob said quietly. "And you've been living with another woman and her child."

"What is this? An inquisition? I know I haven't lived a perfect life like you two have—going to church and all and living your holy-roller life," Kevin shot back. "That doesn't mean I can't be a father to my children."

"This isn't about who is the better person, son," Bob said, unfazed by Kevin's outburst. "This is about the children and being an example to them and being a person they want to emulate. Your father left when you were young. Unfortunately, you did the same to your children. Would you want Sam or Christopher to do the same to any family they have in the future? And how would you feel if your father came to you and said he was sorry and that he wanted to be a father to you now? How would you feel about that?"

Kevin worked his mouth, as if trying to find the right words. "What could I do? I was stuck. Working a dead-end job. Three kids, a wife, stuck in an apartment. I saw no way out." He stopped there, sensing that he had ventured into dangerous territory.

"When I found out that Denise had died, I didn't know what to think. I guess, in one part of my mind, I had always thought I would go back. I'd try to be a father to my kids and a husband to Denise. I'd try to be a family again. But now . . . it's too late."

His voice broke, and for a moment Charlotte felt sorry for Kevin.

But when she thought of all those years that Denise had been on her own, her heart hardened just a little. Kevin had had many opportunities to be a father and husband. Just because Denise died didn't mean he suddenly had to become all the things to them that he hadn't been before.

"How do you want to proceed on this?" Bob asked, his voice even, seemingly unmoved by Kevin's remorse.

Kevin picked up the paper with the figures on it, his eyes flicking over the numbers, as if avoiding Bob's eyes. "I just need a better job, and I can do this." Kevin put the paper down again and sat back. "I could."

He sounds defensive, Charlotte thought.

And it didn't sound like he was going to give in.

"And you've hired a lawyer." Bob picked up the letter they had received, but Charlotte could see the slight trembling in his fingers. Was Kevin going to call their bluff?

Had they done the wrong thing?

Kevin pointed to the paper, and then held up his hands. "I'm not giving up on them."

"Nor should you," Bob said. "You are their father and an important part of their lives. We don't want to take that away from them or from you."

Kevin folded his arms across his chest, rocking in his

chair. "And, well, I may as well let you know now, I'm not going to be around for Christmas. Earlier today I got a call on a job. I wasn't going to take it, but now I think it would be a good idea if I did. Especially if I want to take care of my kids."

Charlotte couldn't help a small feeling of triumph. He wasn't going to have the children at Christmas after all. But right behind that came a niggling sense of confusion. She knew they weren't done with him. Kevin hadn't said he was giving up on trying to get the kids.

"So this letter from the lawyer..." Bob held it up.

Kevin got up and shoved his hands in the back pockets of his pants. "I obviously have some thinking to do, so I'll leave that be for a while. But I'm not sure I'm done with all of this yet."

"So what now?" Bob asked.

"I'll leave you all alone. For now."

Charlotte felt relieved, but at the same time, she wished things could have been resolved more completely.

But does that ever happen, she wondered? Since the children came to live with them, one thing seemed to flow into another, good and bad. It seemed as soon as one thing was resolved another challenge arose.

She knew it wasn't realistic to have Kevin completely out of the children's lives, nor did she want that. But it would have made her feel better to know definitively that she and Bob wouldn't have that shadow hanging over them in the future.

Charlotte caught a movement out of the corner of her eye and glanced at the clock at the same time as she got to her feet. Funny how easily she had slipped into the regular routine of children coming home from school. As they stepped onto the porch, stomping the snow off their boots, she put the water on for hot chocolate, put out cookies, making a welcoming space for them.

And now, as far as she knew, this routine would continue. *Thank you, Lord*, she prayed as she pulled mugs from the cupboard and set them on the counter.

"Hey, kids," Kevin said, his enthusiasm sounding forced as Sam, Emily, and Christopher came into the kitchen. "How are you all doing?"

The children gave subdued replies, and, to Charlotte's great surprise, Sam came over and gave Charlotte a hug. "Hey, Grandma. Do you need a hand?"

Charlotte gave her grandson a quick hug back. "You could put the mugs on the table."

She looked over and caught Kevin watching them; for a moment she wondered about his relationship with his mother. Wondered if Kevin had had grandparents who cared about him.

As the children drank their hot chocolate, Kevin tried to engage them, but the conversation was desultory. Finally, after about fifteen painful minutes, Kevin pushed his mug away and got up. "Well, I suppose I should push along," he said, picking his coat off the back of the chair and threading his arms through the sleeves.

"You're leaving? We don't have to go with you?" Emily asked.

Kevin seemed to wince at Emily's poorly worded question, and Charlotte experienced another moment's sympathy for him.

"No. In fact, I'm sorry to tell you that I won't be around for Christmas."

"Why not?" Sam asked, his gaze flicking upward from his study of his hot chocolate.

"Well, I got a job offer that I don't want to turn down. They need me, so . . ." He spread his hands out in a gesture of defeat. "What can I say?" He gave them all a quick smile as he zipped up his coat. "I guess I'll be pushing off. You kids want to walk me to the porch? Say good-bye to your old man in private?"

Emily and Sam got to their feet, but Christopher stayed in his chair.

Bob gently nudged his grandson. "You should go," he said quietly.

Christopher sighed and shook his head. "I don't think he likes me."

"He's your dad. He loves you. He just has to learn how to show it. That's very hard for us guys, you know," Bob said in a tone that seemed to indicate that Christopher, as a fellow guy, fully understood.

"I guess." Christopher slid off his chair and gave Bob a huge smile. "I'm glad we can stay here for Christmas. I want to go on the snowmobile every day."

"I'm sure you do," Bob said, patting him on the shoulder. "Now go, son. And close the porch door behind you."

Christopher scampered off; as he closed the door, Charlotte could hear murmured voices. Then, ten minutes later, the door to the kitchen and the door to the porch opened at the same time, sending a blast of cold air through the house.

She could hear the loud growl of Kevin's truck starting

up. The children walked to the window overlooking the yard and stood there a moment, watching him leave.

Then Sam turned away from the window. "Can I use the computer? I need to go online."

"It's my turn, Grandma," Emily protested.

"Why do you need to use the computer?" Charlotte asked.

"I'm going to fill out my college application forms," Sam said, shooting a glance over his shoulder.

"Since when are you suddenly motivated to do that?" Emily's question preempted Charlotte's.

Sam shrugged. "I was going to fill in those forms sooner or later. I just needed to be sure. And I'm sure now."

"What made you sure?" Charlotte asked.

Sam pushed his hand through his hair and lifted his shoulders in another shrug. "I guess it was seeing Dad. Listening to him talk about how great his life was, yet he's living in a motel and his credit cards get declined. Doesn't seem so great when you see it up close and personal."

Charlotte didn't respond to that statement, thankful that his father's life had pushed Sam to finally make a decision. "You go ahead," she said with an encouraging smile.

"You can check them when I'm done," Sam offered.

But Charlotte shook her head. "No. I trust you to do the job."

"Besides, she couldn't figure out if you did them right anyway," Bob said with a teasing smile.

Emily sat down at the table and took a cookie from the plate, a soft smile curving her lips. Then she glanced over at Charlotte, and her smile grew. "So I guess we'll be here for Christmas after all," she said.

Charlotte returned her smile and dared to ask, "And how do you feel about that?"

Emily sighed a gentle sigh. "Pretty good, actually."

And pretty good was good enough for Charlotte.

"Can I use the phone, Grandma?"

"Of course."

Emily pushed a pile of crumbs around on the table. "I need to call Ashley."

"Didn't you talk to her at school today?"

"I did."

"And?"

Emily gave Charlotte a crooked smile. "She said she was sorry and that she wasn't being a very good friend."

"And does that satisfy you?"

"Yeah, it does." Emily got up and grabbed the phone. "Besides, we *have* to make up."

"Why is that?"

"Because what am I going to do with her Christmas present otherwise?"

Chapter Nineteen

"And this present is for you," Emily said, handing Pete a shiny wrapped package.

Charlotte pulled her housecoat closer around herself, stifling a slight shiver. The heat from the corn burner hadn't reached her yet.

But that didn't matter, because she glowed inside on this Christmas morning.

The gentle strains of Christmas carols threaded through the rustling of wrapping paper dropping onto the floor and the happy chatter of the kids as they encouraged Pete to hurry up and open his present.

Bob sat beside her, the twinkling lights of the Christmas tree reflecting off his glasses. He was dressed, and it looked like he'd already been outside. Charlotte wondered what he had been doing but didn't ask. It was Christmas, after all. A time of magical surprises and gifts.

The pile of presents under the tree had been shrinking, and now, only one large rectangular gift remained visible.

"Stop wasting time, Uncle Pete," Emily was saying. "Just open it already."

"This is really nice wrapping. I figured I could use it to wrap Dana's present." Pete made a big show of carefully folding the shiny paper.

Emily made a grab for it and Pete looked aghast.

"My name is Pete Stevenson," he intoned in a Spanish accent as he pushed her away. "You stole my paper. Prepare to die."

"I thought we were done with those stupid quotes from *The Princess Bride*," Sam groaned.

"That would take a miracle," Emily said.

From Sam's eye roll Charlotte guessed her comment was another quote from the movie. At Pete and Emily's insistence, she had finally watched the show and was mildly entertained by it but couldn't understand why they would have watched it so much they could quote from it endlessly.

"Okay, Buttercup, here goes," Pete said, opening the box he had been given. He held up a pair of lined leather gloves. "Wow, these are great. Thanks so much." He pulled them onto his hands and flexed his fingers. "And they're nice and warm."

"And you're not allowed to use them to pump gas from the tank into your truck," Emily warned. "They're for wearing to church and for when you take Miss Simons out."

"As you wish," Pete said bowing his head in a mock salute. "And thanks again."

"And now, one last present," Sam said diving under the Christmas tree and pulling out the final gift, hidden in back. He glanced at Emily and Christopher and brought the gift to Bob and Charlotte. "This is for both of you from me, Emily, and Christopher." He looked a bit self-conscious as he handed Charlotte the present.

"Why, thank you so much," Charlotte said, holding the beautifully wrapped gift and glancing at Bob. "I feel like I should save the paper too," she said, running her finger over the shiny wrapping.

"Here. I'll help you get over that." Bob reached over, hooked his finger under an edge and tore it down the middle. "Now you don't have to bother."

Charlotte had to laugh, even as she felt a moment's regret for the desecration of such beautiful paper.

"Okay, okay," she said, ripping the rest of the paper off like a little child.

She uncovered a large picture frame, and as she held it up, she felt a burst of pure, unadulterated love.

Staring back at her from the frame was a collage of candid shots of each of the grandchildren, including baby Will. The pictures were organized in a circle around an older photo of her and Bob.

"Oh, my word," she breathed, touching each of the beloved faces in the grouping one by one. "This is so beautiful."

Bob, leaning over to see the gift, was slowly shaking his head. "How did you children do this?"

"We used Emily's camera to take our pictures," Sam said. "And Anna e-mailed us the pictures of her kids. Then we took them into town to get printed."

"This is so beautiful," Charlotte said, feeling her throat thicken with emotion. "So precious." She continued to touch each of the photographed faces of the children.

Christopher with a little half-smirk on his face, his cheeks red, and his stocking cap pulled on crooked. Emily giving her best flirtatious look. Sam with his arms crossed, standing in front of a snow-covered field, his head bare and his coat open. Will's scrunched-up, newborn face. Jennifer looking like someone had surprised her mid-mischief, and Madison appearing primly amused.

"This is a wonderful, wonderful gift."

"All we have to do now," Emily said, "is get a newer picture of you and Grandpa for the middle." She held up her camera. "Can I take one now?"

Charlotte clutched her hair, knowing what a rat's nest it looked like. "Can we wait until we come home from church? When I have some makeup on and my hair is decent?"

"Of course," Emily said with a laugh. She looked back at the tree. "So I guess we're all done for another year."

"Not quite," Charlotte said, pushing herself off her chair. She stepped over to the Christmas tree and pulled an envelope out of the branches. "There's this yet." She opened the envelope and drew out three smaller ones. "This came a couple of days ago in the mail. From your father."

Silence followed as the children each took the envelopes with their names written on them. Emily opened hers first.

"A gift card," Emily said with a smile. "For fifty dollars at my favorite clothing store."

"I got one for that skateboarding shop." Sam held his up with a grin.

"And I got one for that place where we bought my Nintendo." Chris was all smiles. "I can get another game."

"I hope the certificates are good for the money," Sam said with a wry grin.

"Of course they are," Pete put in. "You can't get a gift certificate if you don't have the money."

Sam nodded, still looking down at the card. "I'm glad he thought of us," he said.

"Of course he would. He's your father," Bob said.

Sam and Emily exchanged a wry look, and then Emily gave Bob a quick smile. "Yeah. I guess."

Sam put his card with his other presents, and Emily tucked hers in the pocket of her pajama pants. Christopher was staring off into space, still holding his. Probably dreaming of what he was going to buy with it, Charlotte thought.

Bob pushed himself off his chair. "If we're done here, I guess I can give my present to you all."

This caught Christopher's attention. "I thought we were all done." He shot a puzzled glance at the empty space under the Christmas tree.

"Well, my present to you is, I already did the chores, so you don't have to do anything else today."

This was greeted with a chorus of thank-yous and hugs from all three children.

Charlotte had to smile. Even after all these years of marriage, Bob could still surprise her.

"But I do have one more thing," Bob said, pulling a piece of paper out of his back pocket. He gave it to Pete, who took it and then frowned.

"What's this?"

"Look at it."

Pete unfolded the paper, read it, shook his head, and read it again. "This is for an appointment with a builder."

"To draw up plans for a house for you and Dana."

Pete's mouth fell open. He blinked and looked from his father to his mother.

"But I thought we couldn't afford—"

"We can, and we will," Bob said.

Silence followed Bob's decisive comment, and Charlotte sent up a silent prayer of thanks that this particular issue was also resolved.

"Well, I better get ready," Pete said, getting up. He folded up the paper and slipped it in his back pocket. "I promised Dana I would stop by her place and take her to church."

"You'll be coming here for dinner, right?" Charlotte asked.

"Do you even need to ask?" Pete said, his question answering hers. "Especially now that we have plans to make." Pete looked over at his father and gave him an awkward hug.

"Thanks, Dad. This means a lot."

Bob nodded, looking a little embarrassed. "I just want you to know how much I appreciate your work. You're a good son, and this was a small way of saying thanks."

Pete looked at the paper again, his smile a mile wide. "I can hardly wait to tell Dana."

Charlotte smiled as Pete sauntered out of the house, whistling, his happiness and general contentment contagious.

"I'm taking my presents upstairs," Christopher said, gathering all his things.

"Don't forget, we've got church later," Charlotte warned,

pushing herself off her chair. "And we're going to have breakfast in about half an hour."

"I'm going to call Arielle. See how she liked her present," Sam said, sauntering over to the phone.

"No fair. You hogged the phone talking to her all last night, making your college plans," Emily protested, scrambling to her feet in a bid to beat him to the telephone. "You can talk to her at church."

But Sam got there first and held the handset aloft.

"Sam Slater. You give me that phone right now." Emily made a futile grab for the handset just as Sam danced out of her reach.

"You can call Ashley when I'm done."

"You won't be done for hours," Emily retorted, making another grab for the phone.

"Hey, you guys," Bob hollered. "Settle down or I *will* find some chores for you to do."

Emily just grinned, knowing her grandfather was teasing. "Sam won't give me the phone."

Bob glanced at Charlotte, who was heading toward the sanctuary of her kitchen, her hands up in a gesture of surrender. "Don't look at me," she said. "I'm not getting between teenagers and the telephone. I've got pancakes to make."

Sam just laughed and raced down the hall and up the stairs, Emily in close pursuit.

Charlotte heard a thump on the landing, and then a wail. "Emily, that hurt," Christopher called.

"Sorry, buddy," she heard Emily say, "Hey, Sam, no fair. Come back here."

"I'll get you for this, Emily," Christopher replied, his footsteps following his brother and sister up the stairs.

Bob snapped open the newspaper and leaned back in his recliner.

"Home sweet home," he said with a sigh. Then he looked over at Charlotte and winked. "And I wouldn't trade it for all the money in the world."

"Neither would I," Charlotte added, smiling in spite of the momentary chaos reigning in their home.

She continued on to the kitchen, humming along to the song playing on the radio.

"... peace on earth, goodwill to men."

And even as the children playfully bickered upstairs, she felt the peace that was promised at Christmas.

She didn't know what was coming in the next few months, the next year. She knew there would be changes as the children grew up and started making their own decisions. But for now, she and Bob had their grandchildren with them, and for now, they were home.

Thank You, Lord, she prayed again as she pulled the bowl out of the cupboard and the eggs out of the refrigerator. *Thank You for our children and our home and the community we live in. Thank You that you gave up Your son.*

For just a moment, she understood what a sacrifice that had been.

Thank You for the promise of Christmas, she prayed as she started working on the next meal for her family.

About the Author

Carolyne Aarsen is the author of over sixty books and counting and not ready to quit any time soon. She lives on a farm close to the hamlet of Neerlandia where she and her husband have raised four children and taken in numerous foster children. She is currently self-published and enjoying that journey far more than she expected.

A Note from the Editors

We hope you enjoyed this volume in the Home to Heather Creek series, published by Guideposts.

For over seventy-five years, Guideposts, a nonprofit organization, has been driven by a vision of a world filled with hope. We aspire to be the voice of a trusted friend, a friend who makes you feel more hopeful and connected.

By making a purchase from Guideposts, you join our community in touching millions of lives, inspiring them to believe that all things are possible through faith, hope, and prayer. Your continued support allows us to provide uplifting resources to those in need.

Whether through our online communities, websites, apps, or publications, we strive to inspire our audiences, bring them together, and comfort, uplift, entertain, and guide them.

To learn more, please go to guideposts.org.